Legal Notice

ISBN-13: 978-1511878180
ISBN-10: 1511878185

D0068204

BOOKS FROM THE GET 800 COLLECTION

28 New SAT Math Lessons to Improve Your Score in One Month
> Beginner Course
> Intermediate Course
> Advanced Course

New SAT Math Problems Arranged by Topic and Difficulty Level

New SAT Verbal Book for Reading and Writing Mastery

320 SAT Math Subject Test Problems Arranged by Topic and Difficulty Level
> Level 1 Test
> Level 2 Test

320 ACT Math Problems Arranged by Topic and Difficulty Level

320 AP Calculus AB Problems Arranged by Topic and Difficulty Level

320 AP Calculus BC Problems Arranged by Topic and Difficulty Level

320 GRE Math Problems Arranged by Topic and Difficulty Level

The 32 Most Effective SAT Math Strategies

SAT Prep Official Study Guide Math Companion

SAT Vocabulary Book

555 Math IQ Questions for Middle School Students

555 Advanced Math Problems for Middle School Students

555 Geometry Problems for High School Students

Algebra Handbook for Gifted Middle School Students

CONNECT WITH DR. STEVE WARNER

www.facebook.com/SATPrepGet800
www.youtube.com/TheSATMathPrep
www.twitter.com/SATPrepGet800
www.linkedin.com/in/DrSteveWarner
www.pinterest.com/SATPrepGet800
plus.google.com/+SteveWarnerPhD

New SAT Math Problems arranged by Topic and Difficulty Level

For the Revised SAT
March 2016 and Beyond

Dr. Steve Warner

Table of Contents

ACTIONS TO COMPLETE BEFORE YOU READ THIS BOOK

1. Purchase a TI-84 or equivalent calculator

It is recommended that you use a TI-84 or comparable calculator for the SAT. Answer explanations in this book will always assume you are using such a calculator.

2. Take a practice SAT from the Official Guide to get your preliminary SAT math score

Use this score to help you determine the problems you should be focusing on (see page 9 for details).

3. Claim your FREE bonus

Visit the following webpage and enter your email address to receive additional problems with solutions.

www.thesatmathprep.com/NewSAT2016.html

4. 'Like' my Facebook page

This page is updated regularly with SAT prep advice, tips, tricks, strategies, and practice problems. Visit the following webpage and click the 'like' button.

www.facebook.com/SATPrepGet800

INTRODUCTION
THE PROPER WAY TO PREPARE

*T*his book is for the revised SAT beginning in March 2016. If you are preparing for an SAT being administered before this date, then this is *not* the right book for you. The PSAT being given in October 2015 will have the new format, so you can use this book to prepare for that test, especially if you are going for a national merit scholarship.

There are many ways that a student can prepare for the SAT. But not all preparation is created equal. I always teach my students the methods that will give them the maximum result with the minimum amount of effort.

The book you are now reading is self-contained. Each problem was carefully created to ensure that you are making the most effective use of your time while preparing for the SAT. By grouping the problems given here by level and topic I have ensured that you can focus on the types of problems that will be most effective to improving your score.

1. Using this book effectively

- Begin studying at least three months before the SAT
- Practice SAT math problems twenty minutes each day
- Choose a consistent study time and location

You will retain much more of what you study if you study in short bursts rather than if you try to tackle everything at once. So try to choose about a twenty-minute block of time that you will dedicate to SAT math each day. Make it a habit. The results are well worth this small time commitment.

- Every time you get a question wrong, **mark it off, no matter what your mistake**.
- Begin each study session by first redoing problems from previous study sessions that you have marked off.
- If you get a problem wrong again, **keep it marked off**.

7

Note that this book often emphasizes solving each problem in more than one way. Please listen to this advice. The same question is not generally repeated on any SAT so the important thing is learning as many techniques as possible.

Being able to solve any specific problem is of minimal importance. The more ways you have to solve a single problem the more prepared you will be to tackle a problem you have never seen before, and the quicker you will be able to solve that problem. Also, if you have multiple methods for solving a single problem, then on the actual SAT when you "check over" your work you will be able to redo each problem in a different way. This will eliminate all "careless" errors on the actual exam. Note that in this book the quickest solution to any problem will always be marked with an asterisk (*).

2. The magical mixture for success

A combination of three components will maximize your SAT math score with the least amount of effort.

- Learning test taking strategies that work specifically for standardized tests.
- Practicing SAT problems for a small amount of time each day for about three months before the SAT.
- Taking about four practice tests before test day to make sure you are applying the strategies effectively under timed conditions.

I will discuss each of these three components in a bit more detail.

Strategy: The more SAT specific strategies that you know the better off you will be. Throughout this book you will see many strategies being used. Some examples of basic strategies are "plugging in answer choices," "taking guesses," and "picking numbers." Some more advanced strategies include "trying a simple operation," and "moving the sides of a figure around." Pay careful attention to as many strategies as possible and try to internalize them. Even if you do not need to use a strategy for that specific problem, you will certainly find it useful for other problems in the future.

Practice: The problems given in this book, together with the problems in the practice tests from the College Board's Official Study Guide (2016 Edition), are more than enough to vastly improve your current SAT math score. All you need to do is work on these problems for about ten to twenty minutes each day over a period of three to four months and the final result will far exceed your expectations.

Let me further break this component into two subcomponents – **topic** and **level**.

Topic: You want to practice each of the four general math topics given on the SAT and improve in each independently. The four topics are **Heart of Algebra, Geometry and Trig, Passport to Advanced Math**, and **Problem Solving and Data Analysis**. The problem sets in this book are broken into these four topics.

Level: You will make the best use of your time by primarily practicing problems that are at and slightly above your current ability level. For example, if you are struggling with Level 2 Geometry and Trig problems, then it makes no sense at all to practice Level 5 Geometry and Trig problems. Keep working on Level 2 until you are comfortable, and then slowly move up to Level 3. Maybe you should never attempt those Level 5 problems. You can get an exceptional score without them (higher than a 700).

Tests: You want to take about four practice tests before test day to make sure that you are implementing strategies correctly and using your time wisely under pressure. For this task you should use "The Official SAT Study Guide (2016 Edition)." Take one test every few weeks to make sure that you are implementing all the strategies you have learned correctly under timed conditions.

3. Practice problems of the appropriate level

Roughly speaking about one third of the math problems on the SAT are easy, one third are medium, and one third are hard. If you answer two thirds of the math questions on the SAT correctly, then your score will be approximately a 600 (out of 800). That's right—you can get about a 600 on the math portion of the SAT without answering a single hard question.

Keep track of your current ability level so that you know the types of problems you should focus on. If you are currently scoring around a 400 on your practice tests, then you should be focusing primarily on Level 1, 2, and 3 problems. You can easily raise your score 100 points without having to practice a single hard problem.

If you are currently scoring about a 500, then your primary focus should be Level 2 and 3, but you should also do some Level 1 and 4 problems.

If you are scoring around a 600, you should be focusing on Level 2, 3, and 4 problems, but you should do some Level 1 and 5 problems as well.

Those of you at the 700 level really need to focus on those Level 4 and 5 problems.

9

If you really want to refine your studying, then you should keep track of your ability level in each of the four major categories of problems:

- **Heart of Algebra**
- **Geometry and Trig**
- **Passport to Advanced Math**
- **Problem Solving and Data Analysis**

For example, many students have trouble with very easy Geometry and Trig problems, even though they can do more difficult algebra problems. This type of student may want to focus on Level 1, 2, and 3 Geometry and Trig questions, but Level 3 and 4 Heart of Algebra questions.

4. Practice in small amounts over a long period of time

Ideally you want to practice doing SAT math problems ten to twenty minutes each day beginning at least 3 months before the exam. You will retain much more of what you study if you study in short bursts than if you try to tackle everything at once.

The only exception is on a day you do a practice test. You should do at least four practice tests before you take the SAT. Ideally you should do your practice tests on a Saturday or Sunday morning. At first you can do just the math sections. The last one or two times you take a practice test you should do the whole test in one sitting. As tedious as this is, it will prepare you for the amount of endurance that it will take to get through this exam.

So try to choose about a twenty-minute block of time that you will dedicate to SAT math every night. Make it a habit. The results are well worth this small time commitment.

5. Redo the problems you get wrong over and over and over until you get them right

If you get a problem wrong, and never attempt the problem again, then it is extremely unlikely that you will get a similar problem correct if it appears on the SAT.

Most students will read an explanation of the solution, or have someone explain it to them, and then never look at the problem again. This is *not* how you optimize your SAT score. To be sure that you will get a similar problem correct on the SAT, you must get the problem correct before the SAT—and without actually remembering the problem.

10

This means that after getting a problem incorrect, you should go over and understand why you got it wrong, wait at least a few days, then attempt the same problem again. If you get it right, you can cross it off your list of problems to review. If you get it wrong, keep revisiting it every few days until you get it right. Your score *does not* improve by getting problems correct. **Your score improves when you learn from your mistakes.**

6. Check your answers properly

When you go back to check your earlier answers for careless errors *do not* simply look over your work to try to catch a mistake. This is usually a waste of time. Always redo the problem without looking at any of your previous work. Ideally, you want to use a different method than you used the first time.

For example, if you solved the problem by picking numbers the first time, try to solve it algebraically the second time, or at the very least pick different numbers. If you do not know, or are not comfortable with a different method, then use the same method, but do the problem from the beginning and do not look at your original solution. If your two answers do not match up, then you know that this a problem you need to spend a little more time on to figure out where your error is.

This may seem time consuming, but that's okay. It is better to spend more time checking over a few problems than to rush through a lot of problems and repeat the same mistakes.

7. Take a guess whenever you cannot solve a problem

There is no guessing penalty on the SAT. Whenever you do not know how to solve a problem take a guess. Ideally you should eliminate as many answer choices as possible before taking your guess, but if you have no idea whatsoever do not waste time overthinking. Simply put down an answer and move on. You should certainly mark it off and come back to it later if you have time.

8. Pace yourself

Do not waste your time on a question that is too hard or will take too long. After you've been working on a question for about 30 to 45 seconds you need to make a decision. If you understand the question and think that you can get the answer in another 30 seconds or so, continue to work on the problem. If you still do not know how to do the problem or you are using a technique that is going to take a long time, mark it off and come back to it later if you have time.

11

If you do not know the correct answer, eliminate as many answer choices as you can and take a guess. But you still want to leave open the possibility of coming back to it later. Remember that every problem is worth the same amount. Do not sacrifice problems that you may be able to do by getting hung up on a problem that is too hard for you.

9. Attempt the right number of questions

Many students make the mistake of thinking that they have to attempt every single SAT math question when they are taking the test. There is no such rule. In fact, most students will increase their SAT score by *reducing* the number of questions they attempt.

There are two math sections on the SAT – one where a calculator is allowed and one where a calculator is not allowed. The calculator section has 30 multiple choice (mc) questions and 8 free response (grid in) questions. The non-calculator section has 15 multiple choice (mc) questions and 5 free response (grid in) questions.

You should first make sure that you know what you got on your last SAT practice test, actual SAT, or actual PSAT (whichever you took last). What follows is a general goal you should go for when taking the exam.

Score	MC (Calculator Allowed)	Grid In (Calculator Allowed)	MC (Calculator Not Allowed)	Grid In (Calculator Not Allowed)
< 330	10/30	3/8	4/15	1/5
330 – 370	15/30	4/8	6/15	2/5
380 – 430	18/30	5/8	8/15	2/5
440 – 490	21/30	6/8	9/15	3/5
500 – 550	24/30	6/8	11/15	4/5
560 – 620	27/30	7/8	13/15	4/5
630 – 800	30/30	8/8	15/15	5/5

For example, a student with a current score of 450 should attempt 21 multiple choice questions and 6 grid ins from the section where a calculator is allowed, and 9 multiple choice questions and 3 grid in questions from the section where a calculator is not allowed.

This is *just* a general guideline. Of course it can be fine-tuned. As a simple example, if you are particularly strong at Algebra problems, but very weak at Geometry and Trig problems, then you may want to try every Algebra problem no matter where it appears, and you may want to reduce the number of Geometry and Trig problems you attempt.

Remember that there is no guessing penalty on the SAT, so you should *not* leave any questions blank. This *does not* mean you should attempt every question. It means that if you are running out of time make sure you fill in answers for all the questions you did not have time to attempt.

10.   Use your calculator wisely.

- Use a TI-84 or comparable calculator if possible when practicing and during the SAT.
- Make sure that your calculator has fresh batteries on test day.
- You may have to switch between DEGREE and RADIAN modes during the test. If you are using a TI-84 (or equivalent) calculator press the MODE button and scroll down to the third line when necessary to switch between modes.

Below are the most important things you should practice on your graphing calculator.

- Practice entering complicated computations in a single step.
- Know when to insert parentheses:
  - Around numerators of fractions
  - Around denominators of fractions
  - Around exponents
  - Whenever you actually see parentheses in the expression

Examples:

We will substitute a 5 in for *x* in each of the following examples.

Expression	Calculator computation
$\dfrac{7x+3}{2x-11}$	$(7*5+3)/(2*5-11)$
$(3x-8)^{2x-9}$	$(3*5-8)^\wedge(2*5-9)$

- Clear the screen before using it in a new problem. The big screen allows you to check over your computations easily.
- Press the **ANS** button (**2ND (-)**) to use your last answer in the next computation.

- Press **2ND ENTER** to bring up your last computation for editing. This is especially useful when you are plugging in answer choices, or guessing and checking.
- You can press **2ND ENTER** over and over again to cycle backwards through all the computations you have ever done.
- Know where the $\sqrt{\ }$, π, and $\wedge$ buttons are so you can reach them quickly.
- Change a decimal to a fraction by pressing **MATH ENTER ENTER**.
- Press the **MATH** button - in the first menu that appears you can take cube roots and nth roots for any n. Scroll right to **NUM** and you have **lcm(** and **gcd(**.
- Know how to use the **SIN**, **COS** and **TAN** buttons as well as **SIN⁻¹**, **COS⁻¹** and **TAN⁻¹**.

You may find the following graphing tools useful.

- Press the **Y=** button to enter a function, and then hit **ZOOM 6** to graph it in a standard window.
- Practice using the **WINDOW** button to adjust the viewing window of your graph.
- Practice using the **TRACE** button to move along the graph and look at some of the points plotted.
- Pressing **2ND TRACE** (which is really **CALC**) will bring up a menu of useful items. For example, selecting **ZERO** will tell you where the graph hits the x-axis, or equivalently where the function is zero. Selecting **MINIMUM** or **MAXIMUM** can find the vertex of a parabola. Selecting **INTERSECT** will find the point of intersection of 2 graphs.

14

11. Grid your answers correctly

The computer only grades what you have marked in the bubbles. The space above the bubbles is just for your convenience, and to help you do your bubbling correctly.

Never mark more than one circle in a column or the problem will automatically be marked wrong. You do not need to use all four columns. If you don't use a column just leave it blank.

The symbols that you can grid in are the digits 0 through 9, a decimal point, and a division symbol for fractions. Note that there is no negative symbol. So answers to grid-ins *cannot* be negative. Also, there are only four slots, so you can't get an answer such as 52,326.

Sometimes there is more than one correct answer to a grid-in question. Simply choose one of them to grid-in. *Never* try to fit more than one answer into the grid.

If your answer is a whole number such as 2451 or a decimal that only requires four or less slots such as 2.36, then simply enter the number starting at any column. The two examples just written must be started in the first column, but the number 16 can be entered starting in column 1, 2 or 3.

Note that there is no zero in column 1, so if your answer is 0 it must be gridded into column 2, 3 or 4.

Fractions can be gridded in any form as long as there are enough slots. The fraction 2/100 must be reduced to 1/50 simply because the first representation won't fit in the grid.

Fractions can also be converted to decimals before being gridded in. If a decimal cannot fit in the grid, then you can simply *truncate* it to fit. But you must use every slot in this case. For example, the decimal .167777777... can be gridded as .167, but .16 or .17 would both be marked wrong.

Instead of truncating decimals you can also *round* them. For example, the decimal above could be gridded as .168. Truncating is preferred because there is no thinking involved and you are less likely to make a careless error.

15

Here are three ways to grid in the number 8/9.

Never grid-in mixed numerals. If your answer is $2\frac{1}{4}$, and you grid in the mixed numeral $2\frac{1}{4}$, then this will be read as 21/4 and will be marked wrong. You must either grid in the decimal 2.25 or the improper fraction 9/4.

Here are two ways to grid in the mixed numeral $1\frac{1}{2}$ correctly.

16

PROBLEMS BY LEVEL AND TOPIC WITH FULLY EXPLAINED SOLUTIONS

Note: An asterisk (*) before a question indicates that a calculator is required. An asterisk (*) before a solution indicates that the quickest solution is being given.

LEVEL 1: HEART OF ALGEBRA

1. Which of the following expressions is equivalent to $5a + 10b + 15c$?

(A) $5(a + 2b + 3c)$
(B) $5(a + 2b + 15c)$
(C) $5(a + 10b + 15c)$
(D) $5(a + 2b) + 3c$

Solution by picking numbers: Let's choose values for a, b, and c, say $a = 2$, $b = 3$, $c = 4$. Then

$$5a + 10b + 15c = 5(2) + 10(3) + 15(4) = 10 + 30 + 60 = \textbf{100}.$$

Put a nice big dark circle around **100** so you can find it easier later. We now substitute $a = 2$, $b = 3$, $c = 4$ into each answer choice:

(A) $5(2 + 2 \cdot 3 + 3 \cdot 4)\quad = 100$
(B) $5(2 + 2 \cdot 3 + 15 \cdot 4)\quad = 340$
(C) $5(2 + 10 \cdot 3 + 15 \cdot 4) = 460$
(D) $5(2 + 2 \cdot 3) + 3 \cdot 4\quad = 52$

Since (B), (C), and (D) each came out incorrect, the answer is choice (A).

Important note: (A) is **not** the correct answer simply because it is equal to 100. It is correct because all three of the other choices are **not** 100. **You absolutely must check all four choices!**

Remark: All of the above computations can be done in a single step with your calculator (if a calculator is allowed for this problem).

Notes about picking numbers: (1) Observe that we picked a different number for each variable. We are less likely to get more than one answer choice to come out to the correct answer this way.

17

(2) We picked numbers that were simple, but not too simple. The number 2 is usually a good choice to start, if it is allowed. We then also picked 3 and 4 so that the numbers would be distinct (see note (1)).

(3) When using the strategy of picking numbers, it is very important that we check every answer choice. It is possible for more than one choice to come out to the correct answer. We would then need to pick new numbers to try to eliminate all but one choice.

* Algebraic solution: We simply factor out a 5 to get

$$5a + 10b + 15c = 5(a + 2b + 3c)$$

This is choice (A).

Remarks: (1) If you have trouble seeing why the right hand side is the same as what we started with on the left, try working backwards and multiplying instead of factoring. In other words, we have

$$5(a + 2b + 3c) = 5a + 10b + 15c$$

Note how the **distributive property** is being used here. Each term in parentheses is multiplied by the 5.

In general, the distributive property says that if x, y, and z are real numbers, then

$$x(y + z) = xy + xz.$$

This property easily extends to expressions with more than two terms. For example,

$$x(y + z + w) = xy + xz + xw.$$

(2) We can also solve this problem by starting with the answer choices and multiplying (as we did in Remark (1)) until we get $5a + 10b + 15c$.

2. Joseph joins a gym that charges \$79.99 per month plus tax for a premium membership. A tax of 6% is applied to the monthly fee. Joseph is also charged a one-time initiation fee of \$95 as soon as he joins. There is no contract so that Joseph can cancel at any time without having to pay a penalty. Which of the following represents Joseph's total charge, in dollars, if he keeps his membership for t months?

    (A) $1.06(79.99 + 95)t$
    (B) $1.06(79.99t + 95)$
    (C) $1.06(79.99t) + 95$
    (D) $(79.99 + .06t) + 95$

18

Solution by picking a number: (We will be using a calculator for this solution)

Let's choose a value for t, say $t = 2$, so that Joseph keeps his gym membership for 2 months.

Now 6% of 79.99 is 4.80 (to the nearest cent). So each month of membership, including tax, is $79.99 + 4.80 = 84.79$ dollars. It follows that 2 months of membership, with tax, is $2 \cdot 84.79 = 169.58$ dollars. When we add the initiation fee we get $169.58 + 95 = \mathbf{264.58}$ dollars.

Put a nice big, dark circle around the number **264.58** so you can find it easily later. We now substitute $t = 2$ into each answer choice and use our calculator:

(A) $1.06(79.99 + 95)*2 \approx 370.98$
(B) $1.06(79.99*2 + 95) \approx 270.28$
(C) $1.06(79.99*2) + 95 \approx 264.58$
(D) $(79.99 + .06*2) + 95 = 175.11$

Since choices (A), (B), and (D) came out incorrect, we can eliminate them. Therefore, the answer is choice (C).

Important note: (C) is **not** the correct answer simply because it came out to 264.58. It is correct because all three of the other choices did **not** come out correct.

* **Algebraic solution:** Since the monthly membership fee is 79.99 dollars, and the tax is 6%, the total monthly fee, with tax, is 1.06(79.99) dollars per month. It follows that the total monthly fee for t months is $1.06(79.99t)$. Finally, we add in the one-time initiation fee to get $1.06(79.99t) + 95$, choice (C).

Notes: (1) 6% can be written either as the decimal .06 or the fraction $\frac{6}{100}$.

To change a percent to a decimal, simply divide by 100, or equivalently, move the decimal point two places to the left, adding in zeros if necessary. Note that an integer has a "hidden" decimal point right after the number. In other words, 6 can be written as 6., so when we move the decimal point two places to the left we get .06 (we had to add in a zero as a placeholder).

To change a percent to a fraction, simply place the number in front of the percent symbol (%) over 100.

19

(2) Since the tax is 6%, it follows that the tax for $79.99 is .06(79.99) or $\frac{6}{100}$(79.99) dollars.

It follows that the total monthly fee, including tax, is

$$79.99 + .06(79.99) \text{ dollars.}$$

We can use the distributive property to simplify this expression as follows:

$$79.99 + .06(79.99) = 1(79.99) + .06(79.99) = 1.06(79.99)$$

(3) See problem 1 for more information on the distributive property.

(4) In note (2) we saw that one way to get the total monthly fee, including tax, is to add the amount of tax to the untaxed amount. A quicker way is to simply multiply the monthly fee by 1.06. A justification for why this works is given in the last line of note (2).

(5) If you need to pay a certain dollar amount more than once, simply multiply by the number of times you need to pay.

For example, if you need to pay 100 dollars five times, then the final result is that you pay $100 \cdot 5 = 500$ dollars. More generally, if you need to pay 100 dollars t times, then the final result is that you pay $100t$ dollars.

In this problem we want to pay the monthly fee t times. Since the monthly fee is 1.06(79.99), the final result is 1.06(79.99)t, or equivalently 1.06(79.99t)

(6) Don't forget to add on the one-time initiation fee to 1.06(79.99t) to get 1.06(79.99t) + 95 dollars.

3. A high school has a $1000 budget to buy calculators. Each scientific calculator will cost the school $12.97 and each graphing calculator will cost the school $73.89. Which of the following inequalities represents the possible number of scientific calculators S and graphing calculators G that the school can purchase while staying within their specified budget?

(A) $12.97S + 73.89G > 1000$

(B) $12.97S + 73.89G \leq 1000$

(C) $\frac{12.97}{S} + \frac{73.89}{G} > 1000$

(D) $\frac{12.97}{S} + \frac{73.89}{G} \leq 1000$

20

* **Algebraic solution:** The total cost, in dollars, for S scientific calculators is $12.97S$, and the total cost, in dollars, for G graphing calculators is $73.89G$.

It follows that the total cost, in dollars, for S scientific calculators and G graphing calculators is $12.97S + 73.89G$.

To stay within the school's budget, we need this total cost to be less than or equal to 1000 dollars.

So the answer is $12.97S + 73.89G \leq 1000$, choice (B).

Notes: (1) When using the symbols "$<$" and "$>$", the symbol always points to the smaller number (and similarly for "$\leq$" and "$\geq$").

(2) To stay within the specified budget means that the total must not exceed \$1000. Some equivalent ways to say this are as follows:

- the total must not be greater than \$1000.

- the total must be less than or equal to \$1000.

- the total T must satisfy $T \leq 1000$.

(3) If the school were to spend exactly \$1000, they would still be within their budget. This is why the solution has "$\leq$" instead of "$<$."

4.   If $-\frac{27}{10} < 2 - 5x < -\frac{13}{5}$, then give one possible value of $20x - 8$.

* **Solution by trying a simple operation:** Observe that

$$20x - 8 = 4(5x - 2) = -4(2 - 5x).$$

So we have

$$(-4)\left(-\frac{13}{5}\right) < -4(2 - 5x) < (-4)\left(-\frac{27}{10}\right)$$

or equivalently

$$\frac{52}{5} < 20x - 8 < \frac{54}{5}$$

So we can grid in **53/5**.

Notes: (1) The simple operation we used here was multiplication by -4.

We simply multiplied each of the three parts of the given inequality by -4, noting that the inequalities reverse because we are multiplying by a negative number.

21

(2) Take careful note of how $-\frac{27}{10}$ and $-\frac{13}{5}$ changed positions when we multiplied by the negative number -4.

(3) If we are allowed to use a calculator for this problem we could multiply each of $-\frac{27}{10}$ and $-\frac{13}{5}$ by -4 in our calculator to get

$$(-4)\left(-\frac{27}{10}\right) = 10.8 \text{ and } (-4)\left(-\frac{13}{5}\right) = 10.4$$

So we can grid in **10.5, 10.6,** or **10.7.**

(4) We actually do not need to worry too much about the inequalities reversing in this problem. We can simply multiply each of $-\frac{27}{10}$ and $-\frac{13}{5}$ by -4, and then choose a number between the two numbers that we get.

5.   The expression $3(5x + 8) - 4(3x - 2)$ is simplified to the form $ax + b$. What is the value of ab ?

* Algebraic solution:

$$3(5x + 8) - 4(3x - 2) = 15x + 24 - 12x + 8 = 3x + 32.$$

So $a = 3$, $b = 32$, and therefore $ab = 3 \cdot 32 = $ **96.**

Note: Make sure you are using the distributive property correctly here.

For example $3(5x + 8) = 15x + 24$. A common mistake would be to write $3(5x + 8) = 15x + 8$.

Also, $-4(3x - 2) = -12x + 8$. A common mistake would be to write $-4(3x - 2) = -12x - 2$.

See problem 1 for more information on the distributive property.

6.   If $x + 7y = 15$ and $x + 3y = 7$, what is the value of $x + 5y$?

* Solution by trying a simple operation: We add the two equations

$$\begin{array}{r} x + 7y = 15 \\ \underline{x + 3y = 7} \\ 2x + 10y = 22 \end{array}$$

Now observe that $2x + 10y = 2(x + 5y)$. So $x + 5y = \frac{22}{2} = $ **11.**

Notes: (1) We can also finish the problem by dividing each term of $2x + 10y = 22$ by 2.

22

We have $\frac{2x}{2} = x$, $\frac{10y}{2} = 5y$, and $\frac{22}{2} = 11$. So we get $\frac{2x}{2} + \frac{10y}{2} = \frac{22}{2}$, or equivalently $x + 5y = 11$.

(2) Although I do not recommend this for this problem, we could solve the system of equations for x and y, and then substitute those values in for x and y in the expression $x + 5y$.

See problem 73 for several different ways to do this.

LEVEL 1: GEOMETRY AND TRIG

7. Given right triangle $\triangle PQR$ below, what is the length of $\overline{PQ}$?

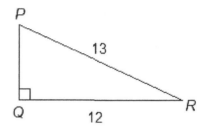

(A) $\sqrt{2}$
(B) $\sqrt{5}$
(C) 5
(D) 7

* Solution using Pythagorean triples: We use the Pythagorean triple 5, 12, 13 to see that $PQ = 5$, choice (C).

Note: The most common Pythagorean triples are 3, 4, 5 and 5, 12, 13. Two others that may come up are 8, 15, 17 and 7, 24, 25.

Solution by the Pythagorean Theorem: By the Pythagorean Theorem, we have $13^2 = (PQ)^2 + 12^2$. So $169 = (PQ)^2 + 144$. Subtracting 144 from each side of this equation yields $25 = (PQ)^2$, or $PQ = 5$, choice (C).

Remarks: (1) The Pythagorean Theorem says that if a right triangle has legs of lengths a and b, and a hypotenuse of length c, then $c^2 = a^2 + b^2$.

(2) Be careful in this problem: the length of the hypotenuse is 13. So we replace c by 13 in the Pythagorean Theorem.

23

(3) The equation $x^2 = 25$ would normally have two solutions: $x = 5$ and $x = -5$. But the length of a side of a triangle cannot be negative, so we reject -5.

8.   What is the radius of a circle whose circumference is π?

(A) $\frac{1}{2}$

(B) 1

(C) $\frac{\pi}{2}$

(D) π

Solution by plugging in answer choices: The circumference of a circle is $C = 2\pi r$. Let's start with choice (C) as our first guess. If $r = \frac{\pi}{2}$, then $C = 2\pi(\frac{\pi}{2}) = \pi^2$. Since this is too big we can eliminate choices (C) and (D).

Let's try choice (B) next. If $r = 1$, then $C = 2\pi(1) = 2\pi$, still too big.

The answer must therefore be choice (A). Let's verify this. If $r = \frac{1}{2}$, then $C = 2\pi(\frac{1}{2}) = \pi$. So the answer is indeed choice (A).

Note: When plugging in answer choices, it's always a good idea to start with choice (B) or (C) unless there is a specific reason not to. In this problem, eliminating choice (C) allowed us to eliminate choice (D) as well, possibly saving us from having to do one extra computation.

* Algebraic solution: We use the circumference formula $C = 2\pi r$, and substitute π in for C.

$$C = 2\pi r$$
$$\pi = 2\pi r$$
$$\frac{\pi}{2\pi} = r$$
$$\frac{1}{2} = r$$

This is choice (A).

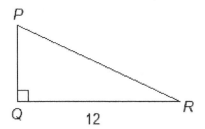

9.   In $\triangle PQR$ above, $\tan R = \frac{5}{12}$. What is the length of side PR ?

    (A) 11
    (B) 13
    (C) 15
    (D) 16

* Since $\tan R = \frac{\text{OPP}}{\text{ADJ}}$, we have $\frac{5}{12} = \frac{\text{OPP}}{\text{ADJ}}$. Since the adjacent side is 12, the opposite side must be 5. So we have the following picture.

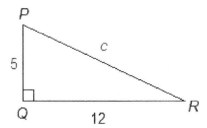

We now find PR by using the Pythagorean Theorem, or better yet, recognizing the Pythagorean triple 5, 12, 13.

So $PR = 13$, choice (B).

Remarks: (1) If you don't remember the Pythagorean triple 5, 12, 13, you can use the Pythagorean Theorem.

In this problem we have $c^2 = 5^2 + 12^2 = 169$. So $c = 13$.

(2) See problem 7 for more information about Pythagorean triples and the Pythagorean Theorem.

(3) The equation $c^2 = 169$ would normally have two solutions: $c = 13$ and $c = -13$. But the length of a side of a triangle cannot be negative, so we reject -13.

25

Here is a quick lesson in **right triangle trigonometry** for those of you that have forgotten.

Let's begin by focusing on angle *A* in the following picture:

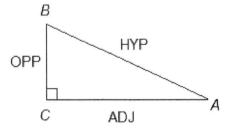

Note that the **hypotenuse** is ALWAYS the side opposite the right angle.

The other two sides of the right triangle, called the **legs**, depend on which angle is chosen. In this picture we chose to focus on angle *A*. Therefore, the opposite side is *BC*, and the adjacent side is *AC*.

Now you should simply memorize how to compute the six trig functions:

$$\sin A = \frac{\text{OPP}}{\text{HYP}} \qquad \csc A = \frac{\text{HYP}}{\text{OPP}}$$

$$\cos A = \frac{\text{ADJ}}{\text{HYP}} \qquad \sec A = \frac{\text{HYP}}{\text{ADJ}}$$

$$\tan A = \frac{\text{OPP}}{\text{ADJ}} \qquad \cot A = \frac{\text{ADJ}}{\text{OPP}}$$

Here are a couple of tips to help you remember these:

(1) Many students find it helpful to use the word SOHCAHTOA. You can think of the letters here as representing sin, opp, hyp, cos, adj, hyp, tan, opp, adj.

(2) The three trig functions on the right are the reciprocals of the three trig functions on the left. In other words, you get them by interchanging the numerator and denominator. It's pretty easy to remember that the reciprocal of tangent is cotangent. For the other two, just remember that the "s" goes with the "c" and the "c" goes with the "s." In other words, the reciprocal of sine is cosecant, and the reciprocal of cosine is secant.

To make sure you understand this, compute all six trig functions for each of the angles (except the right angle) in the triangle given in this problem. Please try this yourself before looking at the answers below.

$$\sin P = \frac{12}{13} \qquad \csc P = \frac{13}{12} \qquad \sin R = \frac{5}{13} \qquad \csc R = \frac{13}{5}$$

$$\cos P = \frac{5}{13} \qquad \sec P = \frac{13}{5} \qquad \cos R = \frac{12}{13} \qquad \sec R = \frac{13}{12}$$

$$\tan P = \frac{12}{5} \qquad \cot P = \frac{5}{12} \qquad \tan R = \frac{5}{12} \qquad \cot R = \frac{12}{5}$$

10. Let $x = \cos \theta$ and $y = \sin \theta$ for any real value θ. Then $x^2 + y^2 =$

(A) -1
(B) 0
(C) 1
(D) It cannot be determined from the information given

* Solution using a Pythagorean identity:

$$x^2 + y^2 = (\cos \theta)^2 + (\sin \theta)^2 = 1$$

This is choice (C).

Notes: (1) $(\cos \theta)^2$ is usually abbreviated as $\cos^2 \theta$.

Similarly, $(\sin \theta)^2$ is usually abbreviated as $\sin^2 \theta$.

In particular, $(\cos \theta)^2 + (\sin \theta)^2$ would be written as $\cos^2 \theta + \sin^2 \theta$.

(2) One of the most important trigonometric identities is the Pythagorean Identity which says

$$\cos^2 x + \sin^2 x = 1.$$

11. A line with slope $\frac{2}{3}$ is translated up 5 units and right 1 unit. What is the slope of the new line?

* Any translation of a line is parallel to the original line and therefore has the same slope. The new line therefore has a slope of **2/3**.

Notes: (1) If we only moved *some* of the points on the line, then the slope might change. But here we are moving all points on the line simultaneously. Therefore the exact shape and orientation of the line are preserved.

(2) We could also grid in one of the decimals **.666** or **.667**.

(3) If the solution is not clear, it is recommended that you draw a picture. Start by drawing a line with slope $\frac{2}{3}$. One way to do this would be to plot points at (0,0) and (3,2) and then draw a line through these two points.

27

Now take those same two points and move them up 5 units and right 1 unit to the points (1,5) and (4,7). Draw a line through these two points.

Note that the two lines are parallel.

(4) Recall that the formula for the slope of a line is

$$\text{Slope} = m = \frac{\text{rise}}{\text{run}} = \frac{y_2 - y_1}{x_2 - x_1}$$

Let's verify that the slopes of the two lines mentioned in note (3) are the same.

For the line passing through (0,0) and (3,2), the slope is $\frac{2-0}{3-0} = \frac{2}{3}$, and for the line passing through (1,5) and (4,7), the slope is $\frac{7-5}{4-1} = \frac{2}{3}$.

So we see that the two slopes are equal.

(5) **Parallel lines always have the same slope.**

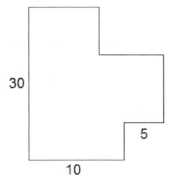

12. In the figure above, adjacent sides meet at right angles and the lengths given are in inches. What is the perimeter of the figure, in inches?

* **Solution by moving the sides of the figure around:** Recall that to compute the perimeter of the figure we need to add up the lengths of all 8 line segments in the figure. We "move" the two smaller vertical segments to the right, and each of the smaller horizontal segments up or down as shown below.

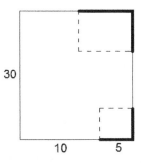

Note that the "bold" length is equal to the "dashed" length. We get a rectangle with length 30 and width 15. Thus, the perimeter is

$$(2)(30) + (2)(15) = 60 + 30 = \mathbf{90}.$$

Warning: Although lengths remain unchanged by moving line segments around, areas will be changed. This method should **not** be used in problems involving areas.

LEVEL 1: PASSPORT TO ADVANCED MATH

13.   If $2x^2 - 11 = 5 - 2x^2$, what are all possible values of x ?

(A) 2 only
(B) -2 only
(C) 0 only
(D) 2 and -2 only

Solution by plugging in the answer choices: According to the answer choices we need only check 0, 2, and -2.

$x = 0$: $2(0)^2 - 11 = 5 - 2(0)^2$ $-11 = 5$ False

$x = 2$: $2(2)^2 - 11 = 5 - 2(2)^2$ $-3 = -3$ True

$x = -2$: $2(-2)^2 - 11 = 5 - 2(-2)^2$ $-3 = -3$ True

So the answer is choice (D).

Notes: (1) Since all powers of x in the given equation are even, 2 and -2 must give the same answer. So we didn't really need to check -2.

(2) Observe that when performing the computations above, the proper order of operations was followed. Exponentiation was done first, followed by multiplication, and then subtraction was done last.

For example, we have $2(2)^2 - 11 = 2 \cdot 4 - 11 = 8 - 11 = -3$ and $5 - 2(2)^2 = 5 - 2 \cdot 4 = 5 - 8 = -3$.

Order of Operations: Here is a quick review of order of operations.

PEMDAS	
P	Parentheses
E	Exponentiation
M	Multiplication
D	Division
A	Addition
S	Subtraction

Note that multiplication and division have the same priority, and addition and subtraction have the same priority.

* **Algebraic solution:** We add $2x^2$ to each side of the given equation to get $4x^2 - 11 = 5$. We then add 11 to get $4x^2 = 5 + 11 = 16$. Dividing each side of this last equation by 4 gives $x^2 = \frac{16}{4} = 4$. We now use the **square root property** to get $x = \pm 2$. So the answer is choice (D).

Notes: (1) The equation $x^2 = 4$ has two solutions: $x = 2$ and $x = -2$. A common mistake is to forget about the negative solution.

(2) The **square root property** says that if $x^2 = c$, then $x = \pm\sqrt{c}$.

This is different from taking the positive square root of a number. For example, $\sqrt{4} = 2$, whereas the equation $x^2 = 4$ has two solutions $x = \pm 2$.

(3) Another way to solve the equation $x^2 = 4$ is to subtract 4 from each side of the equation, and then factor the difference of two squares as follows:

$$x^2 - 4 = 0$$
$$(x - 2)(x + 2) = 0$$

We now set each factor equal to 0 to get $x - 2 = 0$ or $x + 2 = 0$.

So $x = 2$ or $x = -2$.

14. A function $g(x)$ is defined as $g(x) = -5x^2$. What is $g(-2)$?

    (A) -100
    (B) -20
    (C) 20
    (D) 50

* $g(-2) = -5(-2)^2 = -5(4) = -20$, choice (B).

Notes: (1) The variable x is a placeholder. We evaluate the function g at a specific value by substituting that value in for x. In this question we replaced x by -2.

(2) The exponentiation was done first, followed by the multiplication. See the end of the solution to problem 13 for more information on order of operations.

(3) To square a number means to multiply it by itself. So

$$(-2)^2 = (-2)(-2) = 4.$$

(4) We can do the whole computation in our calculator (if a calculator is allowed for the problem) in one step. Simply type -5(-2)^2 ENTER. The output will be -20.

Make sure to use the minus sign and not the subtraction symbol. Otherwise the calculator will give an error.

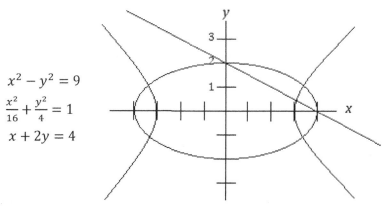

$x^2 - y^2 = 9$

$\dfrac{x^2}{16} + \dfrac{y^2}{4} = 1$

$x + 2y = 4$

15. A system of three equations in two unknowns and their graphs in the xy-plane are shown above. How many solutions does the system have?

    (A) None
    (B) Two
    (C) Four
    (D) Six

* **Solution by looking at the graph:** There is no point that is common to all three graphs. So the system has no solutions, choice (A).

Notes: (1) A solution to the system of equations is a point that satisfies all three equations simultaneously. Graphically this means that the point is on all three graphs. Although there are several points that are common to two of the graphs, there are none that are common to all three.

(2) The graph of the equation $x^2 - y^2 = 9$ is the **hyperbola** in the figure above with **vertices** $(-3,0)$ and $(3,0)$.

(3) The graph of the equation $\frac{x^2}{16} + \frac{y^2}{4} = 1$ is the **ellipse** in the figure above with vertices $(-4,0)$, $(4,0)$, $(0,2)$, and $(0,-2)$

(4) The graph of the equation $x + 2y = 4$ is the **line** in the figure above with **intercepts** $(4,0)$ and $(0,2)$.

$(4,0)$ is the **x-intercept** of the line, and $(0,2)$ is the **y-intercept** of the line.

(5) Consider the following system of equations:

$$\frac{x^2}{16} + \frac{y^2}{4} = 1$$
$$x + 2y = 4$$

This system has the two solutions $(0,2)$ and $(4,0)$. These are the two points common to the graphs of these two equations (the ellipse and the line), also known as **points of intersection** of the two graphs.

(6) Consider the following system of equations:

$$x^2 - y^2 = 9$$
$$x + 2y = 4$$

This system also has two solutions. These are the two points common to the hyperbola and the line. Finding these two solutions requires solving the system algebraically, which we won't do here. One of these solutions can be seen on the graph. It looks to be approximately $(3.1, 0.5)$. The second solution does not appear on the portion of the graph that is displayed. If we continued to graph the line and hyperbola to the left, we would see them intersect one more time.

(6) Consider the following system of equations:

$$x^2 - y^2 = 9$$
$$\frac{x^2}{16} + \frac{y^2}{4} = 1$$

This system has four solutions. These are the four points common to the hyperbola and the ellipse. Finding these four solutions requires solving the system algebraically, which we won't do here. These solutions can be seen clearly on the graph.

Algebraic solution: Observe from the graph that the points (0,2) and (4,0) are intersection points of the line and the ellipse. In other words, they are solutions to the following system:

$$\frac{x^2}{16} + \frac{y^2}{4} = 1$$
$$x + 2y = 4$$

We can verify this by substituting each point into each equation.

(0,2): $\frac{x^2}{16} + \frac{y^2}{4} = 1 \Leftrightarrow \frac{0^2}{16} + \frac{2^2}{4} = 1 \Leftrightarrow \frac{4}{4} = 1 \Leftrightarrow 1 = 1$

$x + 2y = 4 \Leftrightarrow 0 + 2(2) = 4 \Leftrightarrow 4 = 4$

(4,0): $\frac{x^2}{16} + \frac{y^2}{4} = 1 \Leftrightarrow \frac{4^2}{16} + \frac{0^2}{4} = 1 \Leftrightarrow \frac{16}{16} = 1 \Leftrightarrow 1 = 1$

$x + 2y = 4 \Leftrightarrow 4 + 2(0) = 4 \Leftrightarrow 4 = 4$

When we plug each of these points into the equation for the hyperbola however, we get the following:

(0,2): $x^2 - y^2 = 9 \Leftrightarrow 0^2 - 2^2 = 9 \Leftrightarrow -4 = 9$

(4,0): $x^2 - y^2 = 9 \Leftrightarrow 4^2 - 0^2 = 9 \Leftrightarrow 16 = 9$

Since we wound up with false equations, neither of these points are on the hyperbola.

It follows that the system of equations has no solutions, choice (A).

Notes: (1) Although I do not recommend this for this problem, we can solve the following system formally using the substitution method.

$$\frac{x^2}{16} + \frac{y^2}{4} = 1$$
$$x + 2y = 4$$

Let's begin by solving the second equation for x by subtracting $2y$ from each side of the equation to get $x = 4 - 2y$.

We now replace x by $4 - 2y$ in the first equation and solve for y.

$$\frac{x^2}{16} + \frac{y^2}{4} = 1$$
$$\frac{(4-2y)^2}{16} + \frac{y^2}{4} = 1$$

We multiply each side of this last equation by 16 to get

33

$$(4 - 2y)^2 + 4y^2 = 16$$

Now $(4 - 2y)^2 = (4 - 2y)(4 - 2y) = 16 - 8y - 8y + 4y^2$. So we have

$$16 - 8y - 8y + 4y^2 + 4y^2 = 16$$

We cancel the 16 from each side and combine like terms on the left to get

$$-16y + 8y^2 = 0$$

We factor $-8y$ and note that $\frac{-16y}{-8y} = 2$ and $\frac{8y^2}{-8y} = -y$ to get

$$-8y(2 - y) = 0$$

We now set each factor equal to zero.

$$-8y = 0 \quad \text{or} \quad 2 - y = 0$$

So we get the two solutions $y = 0$ and $y = 2$.

We can now substitute these y-values into either equation. Let's use the equation of the line since it's simpler:

$y = 0: x + 2y = 4 \Leftrightarrow x + 2(0) = 4 \Leftrightarrow x = 4$

$y = 2: x + 2y = 4 \Leftrightarrow x + 2(2) = 4 \Leftrightarrow x + 4 = 4 \Leftrightarrow x = 0$

So we see that the two points of intersection of the ellipse and the line are (4,0) and (0,2).

(2) If we wanted to find the intersection points of the line and the hyperbola we would solve the following system as we did in note (1):

$$x^2 - y^2 = 9$$
$$x + 2y = 4$$

In this case however the algebra will be much messier and the solutions do not "look very nice."

It will never be necessary to do such messy algebra on the SAT, so we leave this an optional exercise for the interested reader.

Similarly, for the intersection points of the hyperbola and the ellipse we would solve the following system:

$$x^2 - y^2 = 9$$
$$\frac{x^2}{16} + \frac{y^2}{4} = 1$$

Again, the algebra here is messy, and we leave this as an optional exercise.

16. Which of the following graphs could not be the graph of a function?

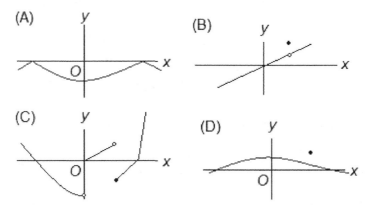

* Only choice (D) fails the **vertical line test**. In other words, we can draw a vertical line that hits the graph more than once:

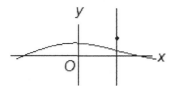

So the answer is choice (D).

$$f(x) = 5x + 3$$

$$g(x) = x^2 - 5x + 2$$

17. The functions f and g are defined above. What is the value of $f(10) - g(5)$?

* We have

$$f(10) = 5(10) + 3 = 50 + 3 = 53$$

and

$$g(5) = 5^2 - 5(5) + 2 = 25 - 25 + 2 = 2.$$

Therefore $f(10) - g(5) = 53 - 2 = \mathbf{51}$.

x	$p(x)$	$q(x)$	$r(x)$
1	5	6	11
2	–3	7	–10
3	–4	–7	3
4	–5	–7	–2
5	–6	0	5

18. The table above gives some values of the functions p, q, and r. At which value of x does $q(x) = p(x) + r(x)$?

Solution by guessing: The answer is an integer between 1 and 5 inclusive (these are the x-values given). So let's start with $x = 3$ as our first guess. From the table $p(3) = -4$, $q(3) = -7$, and $r(3) = 3$. Therefore $p(3) + r(3) = -4 + 3 = -1$. This is not equal to $q(3) = -7$ so that 3 is **not** the answer.

Let's try $x = 4$ next. From the table $p(4) = -5$, $q(4) = -7$, and $r(4) = -2$. So $p(4) + r(4) = -5 + (-2) = -7 = q(4)$.

Therefore, the answer is **4**.

* **Quick solution:** We can just glance at the rows quickly and observe that in the row corresponding to $x = 4$, we have $-5 + (-2) = -7$. Thus, the answer is **4**.

GET MORE PROBLEMS AND SOLUTIONS

Visit the following webpage and enter your email address to receive additional problems with solutions for free.

www.thesatmathprep.com/NewSAT2016.html

LEVEL 1: PROBLEM SOLVING AND DATA

Questions 19 - 21 refer to the following information.

Ten 25-year-old men were asked how many hours per week they exercise and their resting heart rate was taken in beats per minute (BPM). The results are shown as points in the scatterplot below, and the line of best fit is drawn.

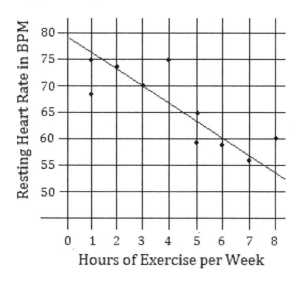

19. How many of the men have a resting heart rate that differs by more than 5 BPM from the resting heart rate predicted by the line of best fit?

    (A) None
    (B) Two
    (C) Three
    (D) Four

* The points that are more than 5 BPM away from the line of best fit occur at 1, 4, and 8 hours. So there are Three of them, choice (C).

Notes: (1) One of the two men that exercise 1 hour per week has a resting heart rate of approximately 68 BPM. The line of best fit predicts approximately 77 BPM. So this difference is $77 - 68 = 9$ BPM.

Similarly, at 4 we have a difference of approximately $75 - 67 = 8$ BPM, and at 8 we have a difference of approximately $60 - 54 = 6$ BPM.

(2) At 5, the point below the curve corresponds to a heart rate that differs from that predicted by the line of best fit by approximately 64 − 59 = 5 BPM. Since this is not *more than* 5, we do not include this point in the count.

20. Based on the line of best fit, what is the predicted resting heart rate for someone that exercises three and a half hours per week?

    (A) 66 BPM
    (B) 68 BPM
    (C) 70 BPM
    (D) 72 BPM

* The point (3.5, 68) seems to be on the line of best fit. So the answer is 68 BPM, choice (B).

21. Which of the following is the best interpretation of the slope of the line of best fit in the context of this problem?

    (A) The predicted number of hours that a person must exercise to maintain a resting heart rate of 50 BPM.
    (B) The predicted resting heart rate of a person that does not exercise.
    (C) The predicted decrease in resting heart rate, in BPM, for each one-hour increase in weekly exercise.
    (D) The predicted increase in the number of hours of exercise needed to increase the resting heart rate by one BPM.

* The slope of the line is the $\frac{\text{change in predicted heart rate}}{\text{change in hours of exercise}}$. If we make the denominator a 1-hour increase, then the fraction is the change in predicted heart rate per 1-hour increase. Since the line is moving downward from left to right, we can replace "change" in the numerator by "decrease." So the answer is choice (C).

*Note: Recall that the slope of a line is

$$\text{Slope} = m = \frac{\text{rise}}{\text{run}} = \frac{\text{change in vertical distance}}{\text{change in horizontal distance}}$$

In this problem the change in vertical distance is the change in resting heart rate, in BPM, and the change in horizontal distance is the change in hours of exercise per week.

38

22. The mean annual salary of an NBA player, S, can be estimated using the equation $S = 161,400(1.169)^t$, where S is measured in thousands of dollars, and t represents the number of years since 1980 for $0 \leq t \leq 20$. Which of the following statements is the best interpretation of 161,400 in the context of this problem?

    (A) The estimated mean annual salary, in dollars, of an NBA player in 1980.
    (B) The estimated mean annual salary, in dollars, of an NBA player in 2000.
    (C) The estimated yearly increase in the mean annual salary of an NBA player.
    (D) The estimated yearly decrease in the mean annual salary of an NBA player.

* When $t = 0$, we have

$$S = 161,400(1.169)^0 = 161,400(1) = 161,400.$$

Since $t = 0$ corresponds to the year 1980, it follows that 161,400 is the estimated mean annual salary, in dollars, of an NBA player in 1980. This is choice (A).

Notes: (1) The year 2000 corresponds with $t = 20$. So the estimated mean annual salary, in dollars, of an NBA player in 2000 would be $S = 161,400(1.169)^{20}$. This is a number much larger than 161,400 (it is approximately 3,666,011).

(2) The function given in this problem is an exponential function. In general, exponential functions have the form $y = ab^t$. Note that $t = 0$ corresponds to $y = a$. In other words, the initial amount is always a.

In this problem $t = 0$ corresponds to the year 1980, and so 161,400 gives the mean annual salary in 1980.

Unlike a linear function, an exponential function *does not* have a constant slope. So in this problem the yearly increase or decrease in mean annual salary cannot be described by a single number.

(3) Let's compare this to the analogous linear function. Suppose for a moment that the equation given instead was

$$S = 1.169t + 161,400$$

In this case, the number 161,400 would still describe the estimated mean annual salary, in dollars, of an NBA player in 1980.

The number 1.169 would describe the estimated yearly increase in the mean annual salary of an NBA player.

23. A biologist was interested in the number of times a field cricket chirps each minute on a sunny day. He randomly selected 100 field crickets from a garden, and found that the mean number of chirps per minute was 112, and the margin of error for this estimate was 6 chirps. The biologist would like to repeat the procedure and attempt to reduce the margin of error. Which of the following samples would most likely result in a smaller margin of error for the estimated mean number of times a field cricket chirps each minute on a sunny day?

   (A) 50 randomly selected crickets from the same garden.
   (B) 50 randomly selected field crickets from the same garden.
   (C) 200 randomly selected crickets from the same garden.
   (D) 200 randomly selected field crickets from the same garden.

* Increasing the sample size while keeping the population the same will most likely decrease the margin of error. So the answer is choice (D).

Notes: (1) Decreasing the sample size will increase the margin of error. This allows us to eliminate choices (A) and (B).

(2) The original sample consisted of only field crickets. If we were to allow the second sample to include all crickets, then we have changed the population. We cannot predict what impact this would have on the mean and margin of error. This allows us to eliminate choice (C).

Technical note: In reality there is a correlation between the frequency of cricket chirps and temperature. You can estimate the current temperature, in degrees Fahrenheit, by counting the number of times a cricket chirps in 15 seconds and adding 37 to the result.

24. A survey was conducted among a randomly chosen sample of 250 single men and 250 single women about whether they owned any dogs or cats. The table below displays a summary of the survey results.

	Dogs Only	Cats Only	Both	Neither	Total
Men	92	14	18	126	250
Women	75	42	35	98	250
Total	167	56	53	224	500

What fraction of the people surveyed who said they own dogs are women?

* There are $75 + 35 = 110$ women who said they own dogs, and there are a total of $167 + 53 = 220$ people who said they own dogs. Therefore, the fraction of reported dog owners that are women is $\frac{110}{220} = \mathbf{1/2}$ or $.\,\mathbf{5}$.

Notes: (1) There are two columns that represent people who said they own dogs: the column labeled "Dogs Only," and the column labeled "Both."

Remember that the word "Both" indicates both dog and cat ownership, and in particular dog ownership.

(2) The numerator of the fraction is the number of women who said they own dogs. There are 75 women who said they own dogs only, and 35 women who said they own both dogs and cats. Therefore, there are a total of $75 + 35 = 110$ women who said they own dogs.

(3) The denominator of the fraction is the number of people who said they own dogs. There are 167 people who said they own dogs only, and 53 people who said they own both dogs and cats. Therefore, there are a total of $167 + 53 = 220$ people who said they own dogs.

(4) This question is very closely related to conditional probability. See problem 115 for more details about this concept.

LEVEL 2: HEART OF ALGEBRA

25. Which of the following expressions is equivalent to $\frac{5k+50}{5}$?

    (A) $k + 10$
    (B) $k + 50$
    (C) $7k + 10$
    (D) $11k$

Solution by picking a number: Let's choose a value for k, say $k = 2$. We first substitute a 2 in for k into the given expression. If we can use our calculator we type in the following: (5*2 + 50) / 5 to get $k = \mathbf{12}$. If a calculator is not allowed, it's not too hard to do the previous computation by hand. Put a nice big, dark circle around this number so that you can find it easily later. We now substitute a 2 for k into each answer choice.

    (A) 12
    (B) 52
    (C) 24
    (D) 22

We now compare each of these numbers to the number that we put a nice big, dark circle around. Since (B), (C), and (D) are incorrect we can eliminate them. Therefore, the answer is choice (A).

Important note: (A) is **not** the correct answer simply because it is equal to 12. It is correct because all three of the other choices are **not** 12. **You absolutely must check all four choices!**

Algebraic solution: Most students have no trouble at all adding two fractions with the same denominator. For example,

$$\frac{5k}{5} + \frac{50}{5} = \frac{5k + 50}{5}$$

But these same students have trouble reversing this process.

$$\frac{5k + 50}{5} = \frac{5k}{5} + \frac{50}{5}$$

Note that these two equations are **identical** except that the left and right hand sides have been switched. Note also that to break a fraction into two (or more) pieces, the original denominator is repeated for **each** piece.

* An algebraic solution to the above problem consists of the following quick computation

$$\frac{5k + 50}{5} = \frac{5k}{5} + \frac{50}{5} = k + 10, \text{ choice (A)}.$$

26. If $i = \sqrt{-1}$, then $(7 + 5i)(-2 - 6i) =$

    (A) 16
    (B) -44
    (C) $16 - 52i$
    (D) $-44 - 52i$

* $(7 + 5i)(-2 - 6i) = (-14 + 30) + (-42 - 10)i = 16 - 52i$, choice (C).

Notes: (1) Here we used the following formula for multiplying two complex numbers:

$$(a + bi)(c + di) = (ac - bd) + (ad + bc)i$$

One option is to have this formula memorized, although this is not necessary (see note(3) below).

(2) Since $i = \sqrt{-1}$, it follows that $i^2 = \left(\sqrt{-1}\right)^2 = -1$.

(3) We can multiply the two complex numbers by using the distributive property and replacing i^2 by -1.

$$(7 + 5i)(-2 - 6i) = (7 + 5i)(-2) + (7 + 5i)(-6i)$$
$$= -14 - 10i - 42i - 30i^2 = -14 - 52i - 30(-1) = -14 + 30 - 52i$$
$$= 16 - 52i$$

(4) We can also use the shortcut of FOILing like many of us do for multiplication of binomials.

$$(7 + 5i)(-2 - 6i) = (7)(-2) + 7(-6i) + (5i)(-2) + (5i)(-6i)$$
$$= -14 - 42i - 10i - 30i^2 = -14 - 52i - 30(-1) = -14 + 30 - 52i$$
$$= 16 - 52i$$

27. If $\frac{3}{x^2+2} = \frac{12}{z}$, where $z \neq 0$, what is z in terms of x ?

    (A) $4x^2 + \frac{2}{3}$
    (B) $4x^2 + 8$
    (C) $4x^2 + 24$
    (D) $\sqrt{\frac{3}{2}x - 2}$

* **Algebraic solution:** We begin by cross multiplying to get

43

$$3z = 12(x^2 + 2) = 12x^2 + 24.$$

We now divide each side of this equation by 3 to get

$$z = \frac{12x^2 + 24}{3} = \frac{12x^2}{3} + \frac{24}{3} = 4x^2 + 8.$$

This is choice (B).

Notes: (1) Be careful to distribute the 12 properly. A common mistake is to write $12(x^2 + 2) = 12x^2 + 2$ instead of $12x^2 + 24$.

(2) Another common mistake is to divide a binomial incorrectly. For example, some students will write $\frac{12x^2 + 24}{3} = 4x^2 + 24$. This is not correct. In other words, in general $\frac{a+b}{c} \neq \frac{a}{c} + b$.

The correct equation is $\frac{a+b}{c} = \frac{a}{c} + \frac{b}{c}$.

(3) Another way to perform the division is to factor first and then divide:

$$x = \frac{12x^2 + 24}{3} = \frac{12(x^2 + 2)}{3} = 4(x^2 + 2),$$

Note however that with the solution above this would create an extra step.

(4) As an alternative, we can solve $3z = 12(x^2 + 2)$ for z by first dividing by 3 to get $z = 4(x^2 + 2) = 4x^2 + 8$. Once again, be careful about distributing correctly at the end.

Solution by picking a number: Let's pick a value for x, say $x = 2$. The left hand side of the given equation then becomes $\frac{3}{x^2+2} = \frac{3}{2^2+2} = \frac{3}{6} = \frac{1}{2}$.

So we must have $\frac{12}{z} = \frac{1}{2}$, and it follows that $z = \mathbf{24}$.

Put a nice big, dark circle around the number **24** so you can find it easily later. We now substitute $x = 2$ into each answer choice:

(A) $4(2)^2 + \frac{2}{3} = 16 + \frac{2}{3} \approx 16.67$

(B) $4(2)^2 + 8 = 16 + 8 = 24$

(C) $4(2)^2 + 24 = 16 + 24 = 40$

(D) $\sqrt{\frac{3}{2}(2) - 2} = \sqrt{3 - 2} = \sqrt{1} = 1$

Since choices (A), (C), and (D) did not come out correct, the answer is choice (B).

44

Important note: (B) is **not** the correct answer simply because it came out to 24. It is correct because all three of the other choices did **not** come out correct.

28. Tickets for a concert cost $4.50 for children and $12.00 for adults. 4460 concert tickets were sold for a total cost of $29,220. Solving which of the following systems of equations yields the number of children, c, and number of adults, a, that purchased concert tickets?

(A) $c + a = 4460$
$4.50c + 12a = 58,440$

(B) $c + a = 4460$
$4.50c + 12a = 29,220$

(C) $c + a = 4460$
$4.50c + 12a = 14,610$

(D) $c + a = 29,220$
$4.50c + 12a = 4460$

* c is the number of tickets sold to children, a is the number of tickets sold to adults, and 4460 is the total number of tickets sold. It follows that $c + a = 4460$.

Since each children's ticket costs $4.50, it follows that $4.50c$ is the total cost for children's tickets.

Similarly, since each adult's ticket costs $12, it follows that $12a$ is the total cost for adult's tickets.

So $4.50c + 12a$ is the total ticket cost, and so $4.50c + 12a = 29,220$.

So the answer is choice (B).

$$\frac{7 - (4 - q)}{8} = \frac{3(5 - q)}{12}$$

29. In the equation above, what is the value of q ?

* **Algebraic solution:** We first apply the distributive property in each numerator to get $\frac{7-4+q}{8} = \frac{15-3q}{12}$.

We then combine like terms in the numerator on the left hand side to get

$$\frac{3+q}{8} = \frac{15-3q}{12}.$$

Now cross multiply: $12(3 + q) = 8(15 - 3q)$.

Distribute again on each side: $36 + 12q = 120 - 24q$.

Add $24q$ to and subtract 36 from each side: $36q = 84$.

Divide each side by 36: $q = \frac{84}{36} = \frac{7}{3}$ or **2.33**.

Note: Make sure you are using the distributive property correctly here. For example, $3(5 - q) = 15 - 3q$. A common mistake would be to write $3(5 - q) = 15 - q$.

An even more common mistake would be to write $-(4 - q) = -4 - q$.

If you frequently fall into this trap, it might help to first rewrite $-(4 - q)$ as $-1(4 - q)$. So we have $-(4 - q) = -1(4 - q) = -4 + q$.

$$
\begin{array}{cc}
5z & 2z \\
4 & 4 \\
4t & w \\
8 & 8 \\
+\,9 & +\,9 \\
\hline
52 & 34
\end{array}
$$

30. In the correctly worked addition problems above, what is the value of $3z + 4t - w$?

Solution by trying a simple operation: Let's rewrite the equations horizontally since that is how most of us are used to seeing equations.

$$5z + 4 + 4t + 8 + 9 = 52$$
$$2z + 4 + w + 8 + 9 = 34$$

We now use a simple operation. The operation to use here is subtraction. Let's go ahead and subtract term by term.

$$
\begin{array}{l}
5z + 4 + 4t + 8 + 9 = 52 \\
\underline{2z + 4 + w + 8 + 9 = 34} \\
3z \;+\; (4t - w) \;=\; \mathbf{18}
\end{array}
$$

Remark: Whenever we are trying to find an expression that involves addition, subtraction, or both, **adding or subtracting** the given equations usually does the trick.

* Visualizing the answer: You can save a substantial amount of time by performing the subtraction in your head (left equation minus right equation).

Note that above the lines the subtraction yields $3z + 4t - w$. This is exactly what we're looking for. Thus, we need only subtract below the lines to get the answer: $52 - 34 = \mathbf{18}$.

Solution by picking numbers: If we choose any value for z, then t and w will be determined. So, let's set z equal to 0. Then

$$4 + 4t + 8 + 9 = 52$$
$$4t + 21 = 52$$
$$4t = 31$$
$$t = \frac{31}{4} = 7.75$$

and

$$4 + w + 8 + 9 = 34$$
$$w + 21 = 34$$
$$w = 13$$

So $3z + 4t - w = 0 + 4(7.75) - 13 = \mathbf{18}$.

Remarks: (1) Any choice for z will give us the same answer. We could have chosen a value for t or w as well. But once we choose a value for one of the variables the other two are determined.

(2) It was actually unnecessary to solve for t above. We could have stopped at $4t = 31$. We then have $3z + 4t - w = 0 + 31 - 13 = \mathbf{18}$.

LEVEL 2: GEOMETRY AND TRIG

31. A rectangle has a perimeter of 16 meters and an area of 15 square meters. What is the longest of the side lengths, in meters, of the rectangle?

   (A) 3
   (B) 5
   (C) 10
   (D) 15

* Solution by plugging in answer choices: Let's start with choice (C) and guess that the longest side of the rectangle is 10 meters long. But then the length of the two longer sides of the rectangle adds up to 20 meters which is greater than the perimeter. So we can eliminate (C) and (D).

Let's try choice (B) next. So we are guessing that the longest side of the rectangle is 5 meters long. Since the perimeter is 16, it follows that the shortest side must have length 3 (see Remark (1) below for more clarification). So the area is $(5)(3) = 15$. Since this is correct, the answer is choice (B).

47

Remarks: (1) If one side of the rectangle has a length of 5 meters, then the opposite side also has a length of 5 meters. Since the perimeter is 16 meters, this leaves $16 - 5 - 5 = 6$ meters for the other two sides. It follows that a shorter side of the rectangle has length $\frac{6}{2} = 3$ meters.

(2) When guessing the longest side of the rectangle we can use the area instead of the perimeter to find the shortest side. For example, if we guess that the longest side is 5, then since the area is 15 it follows that the shortest side is 3. We would then check to see if we get the right perimeter. In this case we have $P = 2(5) + 2(3) = 16$ which is correct.

Algebraic solution: We are given that $2x + 2y = 16$ and $xy = 15$. If we divide each side of the first equation by 2, we get $x + y = 8$. Subtracting each side of this equation by x, we get $y = 8 - x$.

We now replace y by $8 - x$ in the second equation to get $x(8 - x) = 15$. Distributing the x on the left yields $8x - x^2 = 15$. Subtracting $8x$ and adding x^2 to each side of this equation gives us $0 = x^2 - 8x + 15$. The right hand side can be factored to give $0 = (x - 5)(x - 3)$. So we have $x - 5 = 0$ or $x - 3 = 0$. So $x = 5$ or $x = 3$. Since the question asks for the longest of the side lengths, the answer is $x = 5$, choice (B).

Notes: (1) Here is a picture for extra clarification.

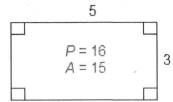

(2) The perimeter of a rectangle is $P = 2l + 2w$.

(3) The area of a rectangle is $A = lw$.

GET MORE PROBLEMS AND SOLUTIONS

Visit the following webpage and enter your email address to receive additional problems with solutions for free.

www.thesatmathprep.com/NewSAT2016.html

48

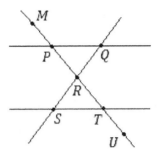

Note: Figure not drawn to scale.

32. In the figure above, $\angle MPQ \cong \angle STU$. Each of the following statements must be true EXCEPT

(A) $\overline{PQ} \parallel \overline{ST}$
(B) $m\angle MPQ + m\angle RTS = 180°$
(C) $\triangle PQR \sim \triangle TSR$
(D) $\triangle PQR \cong \triangle TSR$

* Solution by drawing another representation of the figure: Since the figure is not drawn to scale, let's draw a second representation of the figure, different from the given one, that satisfies the given condition.

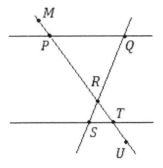

Note that we drew the figure so that $\angle MPQ \cong \angle STU$ is still true. Since $\triangle PQR$ is clearly larger than $\triangle TSR$, we see that $\triangle PQR \cong \triangle TSR$ can be false, choice (D).

Notes: (1) The symbol $\parallel$ stands for "parallel," so that $\overline{PQ} \parallel \overline{ST}$ is read "segment PQ is parallel to segment ST."

(2) $m\angle MPQ$ is read "the measure of angle MPQ." So choice (B) can be read "the sum of the measures of angle MPQ and angle RTS is 180 degrees."

49

(3) The symbol ~ stands for "similar," so that $\Delta PQR \sim \Delta TSR$ is read "triangle PQR is similar to triangle TSR."

Two triangles are **similar** if they have the same angle measures.

(4) In this problem, $\angle PRQ$ and $\angle TRS$ are **vertical angles**. Since vertical angles have the same measure, $m\angle PRQ = m\angle TRS$.

It is also true that $m\angle PQR = m\angle TSR$ and $m\angle QPR = m\angle STR$. See the next solution for details.

It follows that $\Delta PQR \sim \Delta TSR$.

(5) To determine that two triangles are similar, it is sufficient to show that two pairs of angles have the same measure. We get the third pair for free because the angle measures in a triangle always sum to 180°.

(6) The symbol $\cong$ stands for "congruent," so that $\angle MPQ \cong \angle STU$ is read "angle MPQ is congruent to angle STU," and $\Delta PQR \cong \Delta TSR$ is read "triangle PQR is congruent to triangle TSR."

Two line segments are **congruent** if they have the same length. Two angles are **congruent** if they have the same measure. Two triangles are **congruent** if all corresponding sides and interior angles are congruent.

In the last figure we drew, we have $\angle PRQ \cong \angle TRS$ (because they are vertical angles), but $\Delta PQR \not\cong \Delta TSR$.

* Solution by process of elimination: Let's first redraw the picture with just one transversal.

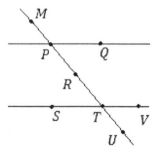

So we have the lines $\overline{PQ}$ and $\overline{ST}$ cut by the transversal $\overline{MU}$ with $\angle MPQ \cong \angle STU$. By the converse to the alternate exterior angle theorem, we have $\overline{PQ} \parallel \overline{ST}$. So we can eliminate choice (A).

50

It then follows that the parallel lines and transversal form 8 angles, any two of which are congruent or supplementary. Since angles MPQ and RTS are clearly not necessarily congruent (in the above figure one is obtuse, the other acute), they must be supplementary. It follows that $m\angle MPQ + m\angle RTS = 180°$, and so we can eliminate choice (B).

Now since $\overline{PQ} \parallel \overline{ST}$, it follows that the alternate interior angles cut by the transversal are congruent. That is $\angle QPR \cong \angle STR$. In the original figure we also have $\angle PRQ \cong \angle TRS$ because vertical angles are congruent. It follows that $\triangle PQR \sim \triangle TSR$, and so we can eliminate choice (C).

Since we have eliminated choices (A), (B), and (C), the answer is choice (D).

Notes: (1) In the last figure above with lines $\overline{PQ}$ and $\overline{ST}$ cut by the transversal $\overline{MU}$, we have the following definitions:

(a) $\angle MPQ$ and $\angle STU$ are called **alternate exterior angles**.
(b) $\angle QPR$ and $\angle STR$ are called **alternate interior angles**.
(c) $\angle MPQ$ and $\angle RTV$ are called **corresponding angles**.

Observe that there is 1 more pair of alternate exterior angles, 1 more pair of alternate interior angles, and 3 more pairs of corresponding angles. Can you find them?

(2) If the lines $\overline{PQ}$ and $\overline{ST}$ happen to be parallel, then the alternate exterior angles formed are congruent. This is known as the **alternate exterior angle theorem**.

(3) There are also two similar theorems for alternate interior angles and corresponding angles.

(4) The converses of each of these theorems are also true. For example, the converse to the alternate exterior angle theorem says "If two lines are cut by a transversal and the alternate exterior angles formed are congruent, then the two lines are parallel.

Can you state the converses to the other two analogous theorems?

(5) To summarize the three main theorems, whenever parallel lines are cut by a transversal, eight angles are formed.

We can split these eight angles into two groups of four. Any two angles in each group are congruent, and if we take two angles from different groups they are supplementary (their measures add to 180°).

For example, $\angle MPQ \cong \angle STU$, whereas $m\angle MPQ + m\angle RTS = 180°$.

(6) Many of the notes from the first solution to this problem are relevant for this solution as well.

33. In $\triangle CAT$, $\angle A$ is a right angle. Which of the following is equal to $\tan T$?

(A) $\dfrac{CA}{CT}$

(B) $\dfrac{CA}{AT}$

(C) $\dfrac{CT}{CA}$

(D) $\dfrac{CT}{AT}$

* **Solution by drawing a picture:** Let's draw a picture.

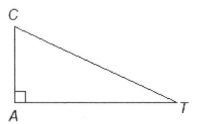

Now just note that $\tan T = \dfrac{\text{OPP}}{\text{ADJ}} = \dfrac{CA}{AT}$, choice (B).

Remark: If you do not see why we have $\tan T = \dfrac{\text{OPP}}{\text{ADJ}}$, review the basic trigonometry given after the solution to problem 9.

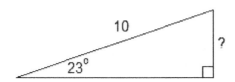

34. As shown above, a 10-foot ramp forms an angle of 23° with the ground, which is horizontal. Which of the following is an expression for the vertical rise, in feet, of the ramp?

(A) 10 cos 23°
(B) 10 sin 23°
(C) 10 tan 23°
(D) 10 cot 23°

* We have $\sin 23° = \dfrac{\text{OPP}}{\text{HYP}} = \dfrac{\text{OPP}}{10}$. So OPP $= 10 \sin 23°$, choice (B).

Remarks: (1) If you do not see why we have $\sin 23° = \dfrac{\text{OPP}}{\text{HYP}}$, review the basic trigonometry given after the solution to problem 9.

(2) To get from $\sin 23° = \dfrac{\text{OPP}}{10}$ to OPP $= 10 \sin 23°$, we simply multiply each side of the first equation by 10.

For those of you that like to cross multiply, the original equation can first be rewritten as $\dfrac{\sin 23°}{1} = \dfrac{\text{OPP}}{10}$.

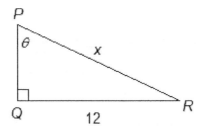

35.　* In the figure above $\theta = 65°$. What is the approximate value of x ?

> (A) 5.07
> (B) 5.60
> (C) 10.87
> (D) 13.24

* $\sin \theta = \dfrac{\text{OPP}}{\text{HYP}} = \dfrac{12}{x}$. Multiplying each side of this equation by x gives us $x \sin \theta = 12$. So $x = \dfrac{12}{\sin \theta} = \dfrac{12}{\sin 65°} \approx 13.24$, choice (D).

Remarks: (1) If you do not see why we have $\sin \theta = \dfrac{\text{OPP}}{\text{HYP}}$, review the basic trigonometry given after the solution to problem 9.

(2) If you prefer, you can think of the multiplication above as **cross multiplication** by first rewriting $\sin \theta$ as $\dfrac{\sin \theta}{1}$.

So we have $\dfrac{\sin \theta}{1} = \dfrac{12}{x}$. Cross multiplying yields $x \sin \theta = 1(12)$. This yields the same result as in the above solution.

36.　* In $\triangle ABC$ with right angle C, $BC = 5$ and $\cos B = 0.7$. What is the length of AB ?

* **Solution by drawing a picture:** Let's draw a picture.

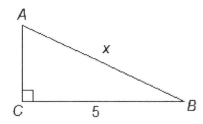

$\cos B = \frac{\text{ADJ}}{\text{HYP}}$. So we have $0.7 = \frac{5}{x}$. Multiplying each side of this equation by x gives us $0.7x = 5$. So $x = \frac{5}{0.7} \approx \mathbf{7.14}$.

LEVEL 2: PASSPORT TO ADVANCED MATH

37. Suppose that $h(x) = 4x - 5$ and $h(b) = 17$. What is the value of b ?

    (A) 4
    (B) 5.5
    (C) 10
    (D) 17.5

Solution by plugging in answer choices: Let's start with choice (C) and guess that $b = 10$. Then $h(b) = 4b - 5 = 4(10) - 5 = 40 - 5 = 35$. This is too big. So we can eliminate choices (C) and (D).

Let's try choice (B) next. So we are guessing that $b = 5.5$. We then have that $h(b) = 4b - 5 = 4(5.5) - 5 = 22 - 5 = 17$. This is correct. So the answer is choice (B).

* **Algebraic solution:** $h(b) = 17$ is equivalent to $4b - 5 = 17$. We add 5 to each side of this equation to get $4b = 22$. We then divide each side of this equation by 4 to get that $b = 5.5$, choice (B).

38. Let a function of 2 variables be defined by $h(x, y) = x^2 + 3xy - (y - x)$, what is the value of $h(5,4)$?

    (A) 76
    (B) 84
    (C) 85
    (D) 86

* $h(5,4) = 5^2 + 3(5)(4) - (4 - 5) = 25 + 60 - (-1) = 85 + 1 = 86$, choice (D).

Notes: (1) This is very similar to problem 14. Everywhere we see an x we replace it by 5 and everywhere we see a y we replace it by 4. Remember to follow the correct order of operations (see problem 13 for details).

(2) We can do the whole computation in our calculator (if allowed) in one step. Simply type $5^2 + 3*5*4 - (4 - 5)$ ENTER. The output will be 86.

39. The expression $x^2 - x - 12$ can be written as the product of two binomial factors with integer coefficients. One of the binomials is $(x + 3)$. Which of the following is the other binomial?

    (A) $x^2 - 4$
    (B) $x^2 + 4$
    (C) $x - 4$
    (D) $x + 4$

Solution by picking a number: Let's choose a value for x, say $x = 2$. Then $x^2 - x - 12 = 2^2 - 2 - 12 = 4 - 14 = -10$ and $(x + 3) = 2 + 3 = 5$. So the answer should be $-\frac{10}{5} = -2$. Put a nice big dark circle around **–2** so you can find it easier later. We now substitute 2 for x into each answer choice:

    (A) $2^2 - 4 = 4 - 4 = 0$
    (B) $2^2 + 4 = 4 + 4 = 8$
    (C) $2 - 4 = -2$
    (D) $2 + 4 = 6$

Since (A), (B) and (D) each came out incorrect, the answer is choice **(C)**.

Important note: (C) is **not** the correct answer simply because it is equal to –2. It is correct because all three of the other choices are **not** –2. **You absolutely must check all four choices!**

Notes: (1) By picking the number $x = 2$, we have changed the problem to "the number –10 can be written as a product of 5 and what other number?" This is why the answer (to this new problem) is –2.

(2) A **binomial** has two terms. For example, the two terms of $(x + 3)$ are x and 3. The two terms of $(x - 4)$ are x and -4.

* Algebraic solution: We are being asked to factor $x^2 - x - 12$. But we are also given that one of the factors is $(x + 3)$. Since $-\frac{12}{3} = -4$, the other factor must be $(x - 4)$, choice (C).

Note: On the SAT, an expression of the form $x^2 + bx + c$ will usually factor as $(x + m)(x + n)$ where m and n are integers and $m \cdot n = c$.

In this problem, $c = -12$ and $m = 3$. So $n = -\frac{12}{3} = -4$.

40. If $g(x) = \frac{x^2 - 4}{x + 2}$ and $a = -5$, what is the value of $|g(a)|$?

We have $a^2 - 4 = (-5)^2 - 4 = 25 - 4 = 21$. Also $a + 2 = -5 + 2 = -3$. We then divide $21 / (-3) = -7$. So $g(a) = g(-5) = -7$. It follows that $|g(a)| = \mathbf{7}$.

Remarks: (1) If you are doing these computations on your calculator, make sure that –5 is put in parentheses before squaring: –5 ^ 2 will give an output of –25 which is not correct.

(2) $g(a)$ can be computed with a single calculator computation as follows:

$$((-5) \wedge 2 - 4) / (-5 + 2)$$

Note that the whole numerator is inside parentheses and the whole denominator is inside parentheses.

(3) We can actually compute $|g(a)|$ in one step with our calculator as follows:

Press MATH, scroll over to NUM, press ENTER (to select abs( ), now enter the expression from note (2), and press ENTER. The display looks as follows:

$$\text{abs}(((-5) \wedge 2 - 4) / (-5 + 2)$$

Note that we do not need the closing parenthesis, although you can put it in if you wish.

(4) I don't necessarily recommend using the absolute value function on the calculator for this. It's quicker to do the computation without this, and then just ignore the minus sign if it appears.

41. Define $[\![x]\!]$ to be the largest integer less than x. What is the value of $[\![\sqrt{75}]\!]$?

* Calculator solution: If we take the square root of 75 in our calculator we get approximately 8.66. The largest integer less than this is **8**.

Solution without a calculator: $64 < 75 < 81$. So $\sqrt{64} < \sqrt{75} < \sqrt{81}$. Since $\sqrt{64} = 8$ and $\sqrt{81} = 9$, we have $8 < \sqrt{75} < 9$. So the largest integer less than $\sqrt{75}$ is **8**.

42. The operation & is defined as $r \,\&\, s = \frac{s^2 - r^2}{r+s}$ where r and s are real numbers and $r \neq -s$. What is the value of $3 \,\&\, 4$?

* $3 \,\&\, 4 = \frac{4^2 - 3^2}{3+4} = \frac{16-9}{7} = \frac{7}{7} = 1$.

LEVEL 2: PROBLEM SOLVING AND DATA

43. * A chemist has a supply of 5.2 liter bottles of a certain solvent that must be shipped to a central warehouse. The warehouse can accept the solvent at the rate of 3 hectoliters per minute for a maximum of 8 hours per day. If 1 hectoliter equals 100 liters, what is the maximum number of bottles that the warehouse could receive from the chemist each day?

    (A) 461
    (B) 462
    (C) 27,692
    (D) 83,200

* The warehouse can receive $3 \cdot 60 \cdot 8 = 1440$ hectoliters of the solvent per day, or equivalently, $1440 \cdot 100 = 144{,}000$ liters of the solvent per day. Therefore, the number of bottles that can be accepted each day is $\frac{144{,}000}{5.2} \approx 27{,}692.30769$. The maximum number of bottles that the warehouse can accept in one day is therefore 27,692, choice (C).

Notes: (1) Since there are 60 minutes in an hour, "3 hectoliters per minute" is the same as $3 \cdot 60 = 180$ hectoliters per hour.

Similarly, since the warehouse can accept the solvent for a maximum of 8 hours per day, "180 hectoliters per hour" is equivalent to a maximum of $180 \cdot 8 = 1440$ hectoliters per day.

(2) In the above solution we combined the two conversions given in note (1) into a single conversion: "3 hectoliters per minute" is equivalent to a maximum of $3 \cdot 60 \cdot 8 = 1440$ hectoliters per day.

(3) Since 1 hectoliter equals 100 liters, we can convert hectoliters to liters by multiplying by 100. So

1440 hectoliters is equal to $1440 \cdot 100 = 144{,}000$ liters.

(4) We can convert between hectoliters and liters more formally by setting up a ratio. The two things being compared are "liters" and "hectoliters."

liters	100	x
hectoliters	1	1440

Now draw in the division symbols and equal sign, cross multiply and divide the corresponding ratio to find the unknown quantity x.

$$\frac{100}{1} = \frac{x}{1440}$$

$$1x = 100 \cdot 1440$$

$$x = 144{,}000$$

(5) Instead of converting 1440 hectoliters to 144,000 liters, and then dividing by 5.2, we can instead convert 5.2 liters to $\frac{5.2}{100} = .052$ hectoliters, and then divide $\frac{1440}{.052} \approx 27{,}692.30769$, giving the same answer of 27,692, choice (C).

44. A psychologist wanted to determine if there is an association between diet and stress levels for the population of middle aged women in New York. He surveyed a random sample of 1500 middle aged female New Yorkers and found substantial evidence of a positive association between diet and stress levels. Which of the following conclusions is well supported by the data?

   (A) A dietary change causes an increase in stress levels for middle aged women from New York.
   (B) An increase in stress levels causes middle aged women from New York to change their diets.
   (C) There is a positive association between diet and stress levels for middle aged women in New York.
   (D) There is a positive association between diet and stress levels for middle aged women in the world.

* A relationship in the given data should only be generalized to the population that the sample was drawn from. In this case, that is middle aged women in New York. So we can eliminate choice (D).

Furthermore, choices (A) and (B) involve a cause-effect relationship. This type of relationship can be established only when the participants surveyed are randomly assigned to groups that are treated differently. In this case all the participants are surveyed the same way. So we can eliminate choices (A) and (B).

The answer is therefore choice (C).

Paramecia present (in thousands) over twelve days

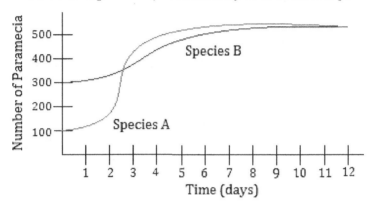

45. A small puddle is monitored by scientists for the number of *paramecia* present. The scientists are interested in two distinct species, let's call them "species A" and "species B." At time $t = 0$, the scientists measure and estimate the amount of species A and species B present in the puddle. They then proceed to measure and record the number of each species of *paramecium* present every hour for 12 days. The data for each species were then fit by a smooth curve, as shown in the graph above. Which of the following is a correct statement about the data above?

    (A) At time $t = 0$, the number of species B present is 150% greater than the number of species A present.

    (B) At time $t = 0$, the number of species A present is 75% less than the number of species B present.

    (C) For the first 3 days, the average growth rate of species B is higher than the average growth rate of species A.

    (D) The growth rate of both species A and species B decreases for the last 8 days.

* The last 8 days correspond to times $t = 4$ through $t = 12$. During this time, the growth rate of both species is decreasing. So the answer is choice (D).

Notes: (1) $300 = 100 + 2 \cdot 100$, and therefore 300 is 200% greater than 100. This eliminates choice (A).

(2) We can also use the percent change formula

$$Percent\ Change = \frac{Change}{Original} \times 100$$

Here the Original value is 100 and the Change is $300 - 100 = 200$. It follows that $Percent\ Change = \frac{200}{100} \times 100 = 200\%$.

(3) To eliminate choice (B) we can use the percent change formula again with Original value 300 and Change $300 - 100 = 200$:

$$Percent\ Change = \frac{200}{300} \times 100 = \frac{200}{3} = 66\frac{2}{3}\%.$$

(4) We can compute the average growth rate over the interval from $t = a$ to $t = b$, by computing the slope of the line passing through the points $(a, f(a))$ and $(b, f(b))$. That is, we would compute $m = \frac{f(b) - f(a)}{b - a}$.

For example, over the first 3 days, the average growth rate of species A is approximately $\frac{400 - 100}{3 - 0} = \frac{300}{3} = 100$ paramecia per day. The two points we used here were $(0, 100)$ and $(3, 400)$.

Similarly, over the first 3 days, the average growth rate of species B is approximately $\frac{350 - 300}{3 - 0} = \frac{50}{3} = 16\frac{2}{3}$ paramecia per day. The two points we used here were $(0, 300)$ and $(3, 350)$.

This eliminates choice (C).

(5) It should be noted that we do not actually need to compute the growth rates to determine which growth rate is higher. We can simply look at the "steepness" of the two curves. An easy way to do this is to draw a "tangent line" to each curve at the point where we wish to examine the growth rate. Here is an example of such an analysis at $t = 2$:

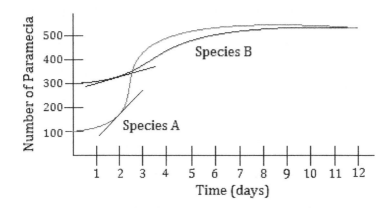

Notice that the tangent line for species A rises faster than the tangent line for species B. This shows that species A is growing faster than species B at time $t = 2$.

(6) We can use a similar analysis as we did in note 5 to see that the growth rate is decreasing for each species between times $t = 4$ and $t = 12$. Here as an example of such an analysis for Species B:

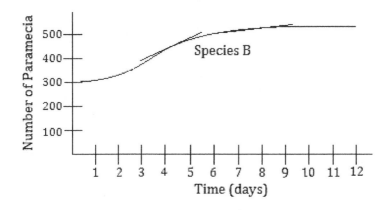

Notice that the tangent line at time $t = 4$ is steeper then the tangent line at time $t = 8$. This suggests that the growth rate of species B is decreasing from $t = 4$ to $t = 12$.

46. * A survey was conducted among a randomly chosen sample of 250 single men and 250 single women about whether they owned any dogs or cats. The table below displays a summary of the survey results.

	Dogs Only	Cats Only	Both	Neither	Total
Men	92	27	5	126	250
Women	75	43	34	98	250
Total	167	70	39	224	500

According to the table, which of the following statements is true?

(A) The number of men that reported they had any pets is greater than the number of people that reported they had dogs only.
(B) The number of people that reported they had any pets is less than twice the number of women that reported they had dogs only.
(C) The percentage of men that reported they had dogs only is less than the percentage of people that reported they had cats only.
(D) The percentage of women that reported they had any pets is greater than the percentage of people that reported they did not have any pets.

* Solution by plugging in answer choices: Let's start with choice (C). The percentage of men that reported they had dogs only is $\frac{92}{250} \cdot 100 = 36.8\%$. The percentage of people that reported they had cats only is $\frac{70}{500} \cdot 100 = 14\%$. Since $36.8 > 14$, we can eliminate choice (C).

Let's try (D) next. The percentage of women that reported they had pets is $\frac{75+43+34}{250} \cdot 100 = 60.8\%$. The percentage of people that reported they did not have pets is $\frac{224}{500} \cdot 100 = 44.8\%$. Since $60.8 > 44.8$, the answer is choice (D).

Notes: (1) Although there is no advantage to starting with choice (C) in this problem, there is *sometimes* an advantage to doing so. Therefore, if there is no specific reason not to, always begin with choice (C) as your first guess (starting with choice (B) would be okay too).

(2) To compute a percentage, use the simple formula

$$Percentage = \frac{Part}{Whole} \times 100$$

For example, from the table we see that 92 men reported that they had dogs only, and a total of 250 men were surveyed. It follows that the percentage of men that reported they had dogs only is

$$\frac{92}{250} \cdot 100 = 36.8\%.$$

(3) There are three columns that represent having a pet – the columns labeled "Dogs Only," "Cats Only," and "Both."

So when computing the percentage of women that reported they had pets, the numerator of the fraction is $75 + 43 + 34$.

(4) For completeness let's check (A) and (B).

For choice (A), the number of men that reported they had any pets is $92 + 27 + 5 = 124$, and the number of people that reported they had dogs only is 167. Since $124 < 167$, we can eliminate choice (A).

For choice (B), the number of people that reported they had pets is $167 + 70 + 39 = 276$, and the number of women that reported they had dogs only is 75. Since $276 > 2 \cdot 75 = 150$, we can eliminate choice (B).

(5) Another way to compute the number of men that reported they had pets is to subtract the number of men that reported they did not have pets from the total number of men: $250 - 126 = 124$.

Similarly, the number of women that reported they had pets is $250 - 98 = 152$, and the number of people that reported they had pets is $500 - 224 = 276$.

47. The average (arithmetic mean) of three numbers is 57. If one of the numbers is 16, what is the sum of the other two?

* We change the average to a sum using the formula

$$\text{Sum} = \text{Average} \cdot \text{Number}$$

We are averaging 3 numbers so that the Number is 3. The Average is given to be 57. Therefore, the Sum of the 3 numbers is $57 \cdot 3 = 171$. Since one of the numbers is 16, the sum of the other two is $171 - 16 = \mathbf{155}$.

Note: The above formula comes from eliminating the denominator in the definition of average:

$$\text{Average} = \frac{\text{Sum}}{\text{Number}}$$

A complete algebraic solution for the advanced student: This method is **not** recommended for the SAT, but it is included for completeness. Let x, y, and 16 be the three numbers. Then $\frac{x+y+16}{3} = 57$. Multiplying each side of this equation by 3 yields $x + y + 16 = 171$. Finally, we subtract 16 from both sides to get $x + y = \mathbf{155}$.

48. To decrease the mean of 5 numbers by 3, by how much would the sum of the 5 numbers have to decrease?

Solution by picking numbers: Let's pick some numbers. The numbers 10, 10, 10, 10, and 10 have a mean of 10 and a sum of 50. The numbers 7, 7, 7, 7, and 7 have a mean of 7 and a sum of 35. So to decrease the mean by 3 we had to decrease the sum by **15**.

* **Quick solution:** One way to decrease the mean of a list of numbers by 3 is to decrease **each** number in the list by 3. Since there are 5 numbers, the sum must be decreased by $3(5) = \mathbf{15}$.

GET MORE PROBLEMS AND SOLUTIONS

Visit the following webpage and enter your email address to receive additional problems with solutions for free.

www.thesatmathprep.com/NewSAT2016.html

LEVEL 3: HEART OF ALGEBRA

49. The daily cost for a publishing company to produce x books is $C(x) = 4x + 800$. The company sells each book for \$36. Let $P(x) = R(x) - C(x)$ where $R(x)$ is the total income that the company gets for selling x books. The company takes a loss for the day if $P(x) < 0$. Which of the following inequalities gives all possible integer values of x that guarantee that the company will not take a loss on a given day?

   (A) $x > 24$
   (B) $x < 24$
   (C) $x > 144$
   (D) $x < 144$

* **Algebraic solution:** First note that $R(x) = 36x$, so that

$$P(x) = 36x - (4x + 800) = 36x - 4x - 800 = 32x - 800.$$

The company will not take a loss if $P(x) \geq 0$. So we solve the inequality $32x - 800 \geq 0$ for x. Adding 800 to each side of this inequality yields $32x \geq 800$, so $x \geq \frac{800}{32} = 25$.

Since we are only looking at integer values for x, $x \geq 25$ is equivalent to $x > 24$, choice (A).

Notes: (1) Income that a company receives is called **revenue**. A revenue function $R(x)$ gives the amount of income the company receives for selling x items.

If the company receives a fixed amount of d dollars per item, then the revenue function is $R(x) = dx$.

In this problem, the company receives 36 dollars per item, and so $R(x) = 36x$.

If the company sells 1 book, then the revenue is $R(1) = 36 \cdot 1 = 36$ dollars.

If the company sells 2 books, then the revenue is $R(2) = 36 \cdot 2 = 72$ dollars.

And so on…

(2) A company's **profit** is revenue minus cost. A profit function $P(x)$ gives the amount of profit (or loss) the company makes (or loses) if it sells x items.

$$P(x) = R(x) - C(x)$$

If revenue is greater than cost, then $P(x) > 0$, and the company makes a profit of $P(x)$ dollars.

If revenue is less than cost, then $P(x) < 0$, and the company takes a loss of $|P(x)|$ dollars.

The **break-even point** occurs when $P(x) = 0$.

In this problem the break-even point occurs when 25 books are sold.

(3) When simplifying $P(x)$, make sure you are using the distributive property correctly. A common mistake would be to write

$$36x - (4x + 800) = 36x - 4x + 800.$$

This error comes from forgetting to distribute the minus sign.

If you frequently fall into this trap, it might help to first rewrite the expression $-(4x + 800)$ as $-1(4x + 800)$. So we have

$$-(4x + 800) = -1(4x + 800) = -4x - 800.$$

(4) In general, $x \geq 25$ and $x > 24$ are not equivalent expressions. For example, if x is allowed to range over all real numbers, then $x = 24.5$ satisfies the second inequality, but not the first.

In this question however we are restricting our x-values to positive integers. In this case, the two inequalities are equivalent.

(5) $P(x) \geq 0$ is equivalent to $R(x) \geq C(x)$. So we could also solve the inequality $36x \geq 4x + 800$. This method of solution avoids having to use the distributive property. We simply subtract $4x$ from each side of the inequality to get $32x \geq 800$, and then divide by 32 to get $x \geq 25$.

Solution by picking a number: Using the answer choices as a guide, let's choose a value for x, say $x = 50$.

Then $R(x) = R(50) = 36 \cdot 50 = 1800$, and

$$C(x) = C(50) = 4 \cdot 50 + 800 = 200 + 800 = 1000.$$

So $P(x) = R(x) - C(x) = 1800 - 1000 = 800.$

So, for $x = 50$, the company *does not* take a loss. Therefore $x = 50$ should be a solution to the inequality. So we can eliminate choices (B) and (C).

We still need to decide if the answer is choice (A) or (D). So let's pick another number, say $x = 20$.

Then $R(x) = R(20) = 36 \cdot 20 = 720$, and

$$C(x) = C(20) = 4 \cdot 20 + 800 = 80 + 800 = 880.$$

So $P(x) = R(x) - C(x) = 720 - 880 = -160$.

So, for $x = 20$, the company *does* take a loss. Therefore $x = 20$ should *not* be a solution to the inequality. So we can eliminate choice (D), and therefore the answer is choice (A).

50. If $y = k^{-\frac{2}{3}}$, where $k > y > 0$, which of the following equations gives k in terms of y ?

   (A) $k = -\sqrt[3]{y^2}$

   (B) $k = -\sqrt{y^3}$

   (C) $k = \dfrac{1}{\sqrt[3]{y^2}}$

   (D) $k = \dfrac{1}{\sqrt{y^3}}$

Algebraic solution: We raise each side of the equation $y = k^{-\frac{2}{3}}$ to the $-\frac{3}{2}$ power to get $y^{-\frac{3}{2}} = \left(k^{-\frac{2}{3}}\right)^{-\frac{3}{2}} = k^{\left(\frac{-2}{3}\right)\left(\frac{-3}{2}\right)} = k^1 = k$. It follows that $k = y^{-\frac{3}{2}} = \dfrac{1}{y^{\frac{3}{2}}} = \dfrac{1}{\sqrt{y^3}}$, choice (D).

Notes: (1) For the laws of exponents used here, see the table below.

For example, we used the law $(x^a)^b = x^{ab}$ to get $\left(k^{-\frac{2}{3}}\right)^{-\frac{3}{2}} = k^{\left(\frac{-2}{3}\right)\left(\frac{-3}{2}\right)}$.

(2) To get rid of an exponent, we raise to the reciprocal exponent. The reciprocal of $\frac{a}{b}$ is $\frac{b}{a}$. Observe that $\left(x^{\frac{a}{b}}\right)^{\frac{b}{a}} = x^{\left(\frac{a}{b}\right)\left(\frac{b}{a}\right)} = x^1 = x$.

The reciprocal of $-\frac{3}{2}$ is $-\frac{2}{3}$. So we have $\left(k^{-\frac{2}{3}}\right)^{-\frac{3}{2}} = k^{\left(\frac{-2}{3}\right)\left(\frac{-3}{2}\right)} = k^1 = k$.

67

(3) We can change a negative exponent to a positive exponent by taking a reciprocal. In this problem, we have $y^{-\frac{3}{2}} = \dfrac{1}{y^{\frac{3}{2}}}$.

A common mistake is to write $y^{-\frac{3}{2}} = -y^{\frac{3}{2}}$. This is completely false. The expression on the left hand side is positive, whereas the expression on the right is negative.

(4) In the expression $a^{\frac{b}{c}}$, a is the base, b is the power, and c is the root. So we can write $a^{\frac{b}{c}} = \sqrt[c]{a^b}$.

For example, $y^{\frac{3}{2}} = \sqrt{y^3}$.

It follows that $y^{-\frac{3}{2}} = \dfrac{1}{y^{\frac{3}{2}}} = \dfrac{1}{\sqrt{y^3}}$.

Laws of Exponents: For those students that have forgotten, here is a brief review of the laws of exponents needed here:

Law	Example
$x^0 = 1$	$3^0 = 1$
$x^1 = x$	$9^1 = 9$
$x^a x^b = x^{a+b}$	$x^3 x^5 = x^8$
$x^a/x^b = x^{a-b}$	$x^{11}/x^4 = x^7$
$(x^a)^b = x^{ab}$	$(x^5)^3 = x^{15}$
$(xy)^a = x^a y^a$	$(xy)^4 = x^4 y^4$
$(x/y)^a = x^a/y^a$	$(x/y)^6 = x^6/y^6$
$x^{-1} = 1/x$	$3^{-1} = 1/3$
$x^{-a} = 1/x^a$	$9^{-2} = 1/81$
$x^{1/n} = \sqrt[n]{x}$	$x^{1/3} = \sqrt[3]{x}$
$x^{m/n} = \sqrt[n]{x^m} = \left(\sqrt[n]{x}\right)^m$	$x^{9/2} = \sqrt{x^9} = \left(\sqrt{x}\right)^9$

Solution by picking a number: Let's choose a value for k, say $k = 8$. Then $y = 8^{-\frac{2}{3}} = \dfrac{1}{8^{\frac{2}{3}}} = \dfrac{1}{\left(\sqrt[3]{8}\right)^2} = \dfrac{1}{2^2} = \dfrac{1}{4}$. So, when we substitute $\frac{1}{4}$ in for y, we should get $k = \mathbf{8}$. Put a nice big, dark circle around the number 8 so you can find it easily later.

We now substitute $y = \dfrac{1}{4}$ into each answer choice:

(A) $k = -\sqrt[3]{\left(\frac{1}{4}\right)^2} < 0$

(B) $k = -\sqrt{\left(\frac{1}{4}\right)^3} < 0$

(C) $k = \dfrac{1}{\sqrt[3]{\left(\frac{1}{4}\right)^2}} = \dfrac{1}{\sqrt[3]{\frac{1}{16}}} = \sqrt[3]{16} < \sqrt[3]{27} = 3 < 8$

(D) $k = \dfrac{1}{\sqrt{\left(\frac{1}{4}\right)^3}} = \dfrac{1}{\sqrt{\frac{1}{64}}} = \sqrt{64} = 8$

Since choices (A), (B), and (C) did not come out correct, the answer is choice (D).

Notes: (1) Since we are plugging y values into the answer choices, we would normally pick a value for y. In this problem we chose a value for k instead because it is much easier to choose k and find y, than it is to do it the other way around.

(2) Note that we picked the number 8 for k, as opposed to an integer like 2. This is because 8 is a perfect cube, and the denominator in the exponent indicates that we will need to take a cube root.

(3) We can change a negative exponent to a positive exponent by taking a reciprocal. In this problem, we have $8^{-\frac{2}{3}} = \dfrac{1}{8^{\frac{2}{3}}}$.

A common mistake is to write $8^{-\frac{2}{3}} = -8^{\frac{2}{3}}$. This is completely false. The number on the left hand side is positive, whereas the number on the right is negative.

(4) In the expression $a^{\frac{b}{c}}$, a is the base, b is the power, and c is the root. So we can write $a^{\frac{b}{c}} = \sqrt[c]{a^b}$.

For example, $8^{\frac{2}{3}} = \sqrt[3]{8^2}$.

It follows that $8^{-\frac{2}{3}} = \dfrac{1}{8^{\frac{2}{3}}} = \dfrac{1}{\sqrt[3]{8^2}}$.

In general, $\sqrt[c]{a^b} = \left(\sqrt[c]{a}\right)^b$. It is often easier to take the root first.

In this problem we have $\sqrt[3]{8^2} = \left(\sqrt[3]{8}\right)^2 = 2^2 = 4$.

(5) There is no reason to continue evaluating answer choices once it is clear that the choice will not yield the correct answer. For example, we see right away that choices (A) and (B) will give negative answers. Since we know our answer should be positive, we can eliminate them.

(6) If we are allowed to use a calculator for this problem, we could use it to evaluate the given expression and compute the answer choices quickly.

For example, given that we chose $k = 8$, we can compute $y = k^{-\frac{2}{3}}$, easily by typing 8 ^ (-2/3) ENTER into our calculator. The display will show .25.

We can then substitute .25 in for y in each answer choice and eliminate any answers that do not come out to 8.

(7) When using the strategy of picking numbers it is very important that we check every answer choice. It is possible for more than one choice to come out to the correct answer. We would then need to pick a new number to try to eliminate all but one choice.

51. For all real numbers x and y, $|x - y|$ is equivalent to which of the following?

   (A) $x + y$
   (B) $\sqrt{x - y}$
   (C) $(x - y)^2$
   (D) $\sqrt{(x - y)^2}$

* **Solution using the definition of absolute value:** One definition of the absolute value of x is $|x| = \sqrt{x^2}$. So $|x - y| = \sqrt{(x - y)^2}$, choice (D).

Note: Here we have simply replaced x by $x - y$ on both sides of the equation $|x| = \sqrt{x^2}$.

Solution by picking numbers: Let's choose values for x and y, let's say $x = 2$ and $y = 5$. Then $|x - y| = |2 - 5| = |-3| = \mathbf{3}$.

Put a nice big dark circle around **3** so you can find it easily later. We now substitute $x = 2$ and $y = 5$ into each answer choice:

   (A) 7
   (B) $\sqrt{-3}$
   (C) $(-3)^2 = 9$
   (D) $\sqrt{(-3)^2} = \sqrt{9} = 3$

Since A, B and C each came out incorrect, we can eliminate them. So the answer is choice **D**.

52. If $\frac{1}{5}x + \frac{1}{7}y = 3$, what is the value of $7x + 5y$?

* Solution by trying a simple operation: We multiply each side of the equation by 35 to get $7x + 5y = \mathbf{105}$.

Remarks: (1) When we multiply the left hand side by 35, we have to multiply **each** term by 35.

$$35\left(\frac{1}{5}x\right) = 7x \qquad 35\left(\frac{1}{7}y\right) = 5y$$

(2) 35 is a natural "first guess" because it is the **least common multiple** of 5 and 7 (it is actually also the **product** of 5 and 7, but I mention the least common multiple here because it is usually the better guess when the two are not equal).

(3) Since 5 and 7 are prime, and therefore have no prime factors in common, the least common multiple of 5 and 7 is the same as the product of 5 and 7.

Solution using a "standard substitution trick": We attempt to change the left hand side of the given equation by putting in what we need. Next to the x we need a 7 and next to the y we need a 5.

$$\frac{1}{5} \cdot \frac{1}{7}(7x) + \frac{1}{7} \cdot \frac{1}{5}(5y) = 3$$

$$\frac{1}{35}(7x) + \frac{1}{35}(5y) = 3$$

$$\frac{1}{35}(7x + 5y) = 3$$

Note that the expression we are looking for is now in parentheses. So we simply multiply each side of the equation by 35 to get

$$7x + 5y = 3 \cdot 35 = \mathbf{105}$$

Remarks: (1) Note that we undo multiplying x by 7 by also multiplying by $\frac{1}{7}$. Similarly, we undo multiplying y by 5 by also multiplying by $\frac{1}{5}$.

(2) We group the $\frac{1}{7}$ with the $\frac{1}{5}$ and leave $7x$ by itself. We can do this because multiplication of real numbers is **associative**. Similarly, for y.

71

53. Gary takes a New York City cab 6 miles to work and must pay $17.50 for the cab ride. After work, Gary takes another New York City cab 10 miles to visit his family and must pay $27.50. During both of these rides, Gary was charged a "drop fee" (an initial charge when the cab's meter is activated) of d dollars, plus an additional m dollars for each $\frac{1}{5}$ of a mile travelled. What is the value of md ?

* We can model the information here with a linear equation $C = mx + d$, where m is the cost of the cab ride per $\frac{1}{5}$ mile, d is the drop fee, and C is the total cost for a cab that travels $\frac{x}{5}$ miles.

We are essentially given two points on the line, but we should convert miles to $\frac{1}{5}$ miles as we write down the points. So 6 miles is equivalent to an x-value of $6 \cdot 5 = 30$ units of $\frac{1}{5}$ miles, and 10 miles is equivalent to an x-value of $10 \cdot 5 = 50$ units of $\frac{1}{5}$ miles. It follows that the two points given are $(30,17.50)$ and $(50,27.50)$.

We can now find the slope of the line passing through these two points:
$$m = \frac{27.50-17.50}{50-30} = \frac{10}{20} = .50.$$

Using the point $(30,17.50)$ and the slope $m = .5$ we can now write an equation of the line in point-slope form: $C - 17.50 = .5(x - 30)$.

Distributing the .5 on the right hand side of the equation gives us $C - 17.50 = .5x - 15$, and then adding 17.50 to each side of this last equation gives us $C = .5x + 2.50$.

It follows that $m = .5$ and $d = 2.50$. So $md = \mathbf{1.25}$ or $\mathbf{5/4}$.

Notes: (1) The slope of a line passing through the points (x_1, y_1) and (x_2, y_2) is

$$\text{Slope} = m = \frac{rise}{run} = \frac{y_2 - y_1}{x_2 - x_1}$$

In this problem the two points are $(30,17.50)$ and $(50,27.50)$.

(2) Using the points $(6,17.50)$ and $(10,27.50)$ would have led to a wrong answer (unless a conversion was done at the end) because x is being measured in $\frac{1}{5}$ miles and not miles.

72

(3) The **slope-intercept form of an equation of a line** is $y = mx + b$ where m is the slope of the line and b is the y-coordinate of the y-intercept, i.e. the point $(0, b)$ is on the line. Note that this point lies on the y-axis.

In this problem we used the letter C (for *cost*) instead of y, and d (for *drop*) instead of b.

It turned out that $m = .5$ and $d = 2.50$

(4) The **point-slope form of an equation of a line** is

$$y - y_0 = m(x - x_0)$$

where m is the slope of the line and (x_0, y_0) is any point on the line.

In this problem $m = .5$ and $(x_0, y_0) = (30, 17.50)$.

(5) We could have used the point $(50, 27.50)$ instead when writing an equation of the line in point-slope form. In this case we would get $C - 27.50 = .5(x - 50)$. I leave it to the reader to show that when you solve this equation for C you get the same slope-intercept form as before.

(6) As an alternative to using point-slope form, after finding m, we could plug one of the points into the slope-intercept form of the equation and solve for d as follows:

$$C = .5x + d$$
$$17.50 = .5(30) + d$$
$$17.50 = 15 + d$$
$$d = 17.50 - 15 = 2.5$$

We now have $m = .5$ and $d = 2.5$, so that $md = 1.25$ or $5/4$.

(7) If we were to take our points as $(6, 17.50)$ and $(10, 27.50)$, we would get a slope of $m = \frac{27.50 - 17.50}{10 - 6} = \frac{10}{4} = 2.50$. This is the cost per mile. We can change this to the cost per $\frac{1}{5}$ mile by dividing by 5 to get $\frac{2.50}{5} = .5$ as before.

(8) **Technical note:** In reality a New York City cab also charges m dollars for each 60 seconds of "wait time" when the cab is stuck in traffic. The question given here avoided this extra complication.

54. If $2x + 3y = 5$, $2y + z = 3$, and $x + 5y + z = 3$, then $x =$

* **Solution by performing simple operations:** We add the first two equations and subtract the second equation to get $x = 5 + 3 - 3 = $ **5**.

Computations in detail: We add the first two equations:

$$
\begin{array}{r}
2x + 3y = 5 \\
2y + z = 3 \\
\hline
2x + 5y + z = 8
\end{array}
$$

We then subtract the third equation from this result:

$$
\begin{array}{r}
2x + 5y + z = 8 \\
x + 5y + z = 3 \\
\hline
x = 5
\end{array}
$$

Solution using Gauss-Jordan reduction: We will need to use our graphing calculator for this solution.

Let's write the system of equations vertically:

$$
\begin{array}{r}
2x + 3y = 5 \\
2y + z = 3 \\
x + 5y + z = 3
\end{array}
$$

The **augmented matrix** for this system is

$$
\begin{bmatrix}
2 & 3 & 0 & 5 \\
0 & 2 & 1 & 3 \\
1 & 5 & 1 & 3
\end{bmatrix}
$$

Push the MATRIX button, scroll over to EDIT and then select [A] (or press 1). We will be inputting a 3×4 matrix, so press 3 ENTER 4 ENTER. Then enter the numbers 2, 3, 0 and 5 for the first row, 0, 2, 1 and 3 for the second row, and 1, 5, 1 and 3 for the third row.

Now push the QUIT button (2ND MODE) to get a blank screen. Press MATRIX again. This time scroll over to MATH and select rref((or press B). Then press MATRIX again and select [A] (or press 1) and press ENTER.

The display will show the following.

$$
\begin{bmatrix}
[1\,0\,0 & 5 &] \\
[0\,1\,0 & -1.67 &] \\
[0\,0\,1 & 6.33 &]]
\end{bmatrix}
$$

The first line is interpreted as $x = $ **5**.

74

Notes: (1) We began by creating the **augmented matrix** for the system of equations. This is simply an array of numbers which contains the coefficients of the variables together with the right hand sides of the equations.

(2) We then put the matrix into **reduced row echelon form** (rref). In this form we can read off the solution to the original system of equations.

Warning: Be careful to use the rref(button (2 r's), and not the ref(button (which has only one r).

LEVEL 3: GEOMETRY AND TRIG

55. The area of a rectangular garden is 448 square feet. A statue with a rectangular base that is twice as long as it is wide is placed in the center of the garden so that the garden extends 6 feet beyond the base of the statue on the top and bottom and 4 feet beyond the base of the statue on the left and right sides. How many feet wide is the base of the statue?

   (A) 6
   (B) 8
   (C) 14
   (D) 20

Let's draw a picture.

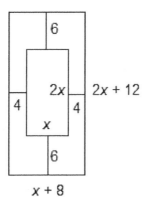

In this picture the larger rectangle represents the garden and the smaller rectangle inside represents the statue.

If we let x be the width of the statue, then the length is $2x$ (since the statue is twice as long as it is wide). Since the garden extends 6 feet beyond the statue on top and bottom, the length of the garden is $2x + 6 + 6 = 2x + 12$ feet. Since the garden extends 4 feet beyond the statue on the left and the right, the width of the garden is $x + 4 + 4 = x + 8$ feet.

It follows that the area of the garden is $(x + 8)(2x + 12)$. We need to find the value of x that makes this expression 448. Here are two ways we can do this:

* Method 1 – Plugging in answer choices: Let's start with choice (C) and guess that $x = 14$. It follows that

$$(x + 8)(2x + 12) = (14 + 8)(2 \cdot 14 + 12) = 22 \cdot 40 = 880.$$

This is too big so we can eliminate choices (C) and (D).

Let's try choice (B) next and guess that $x = 8$. It follows that

$$(x + 8)(2x + 12) = (8 + 8)(2 \cdot 8 + 12) = 16 \cdot 28 = 448.$$

This is correct. So the answer is choice (B).

Method 2 – Solving a quadratic equation: We need to solve the equation $(x + 8)(2x + 12) = 448$. Multiplying out the left hand side gives $2x^2 + 12x + 16x + 96 = 448$. Dividing by 2 gives $x^2 + 6x + 8x + 48 = 224$. We now combine like terms on the left to get $x^2 + 14x + 48 = 224$. Subtract 224 from each side and we have $x^2 + 14x - 176 = 0$. The left hand side can be factored to get $(x - 8)(x + 22) = 0$. So we have $x - 8 = 0$ or $x + 22 = 0$. Therefore, $x = 8$ or $x = -22$. We reject the negative solution to get $x = 8$, choice (B).

Notes: (1) As you can see from method 2, a complete algebraic solution is quite tedious here. Plugging in is a better choice for most students.

(2) We can also plug in answer choices right at the beginning of the problem before doing any algebra at all.

(3) The equation $x^2 + 14x - 176 = 0$ can be solved several different ways. We did it by factoring above, but completing the square and using the quadratic formula are two other alternatives.

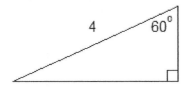

56. The figure above shows a right triangle whose hypotenuse is 4 feet long. How many feet long is the shorter leg of this triangle?

(A) 2

(B) 8

(C) $2\sqrt{3}$

(D) $\frac{2\sqrt{3}}{3}$

* **Solution using a 30, 60, 90 right triangle:** The following figure is given at the beginning of each math section on the SAT.

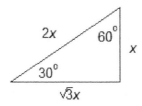

Comparing the figure given in the problem to this figure, we see that $2x = 4$ and so $x = 2$, choice (A).

Note: For the SAT, the following two special triangles are given at the beginning of each math section:

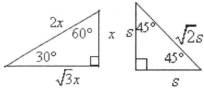

Some students get a bit confused because there are variables in these pictures. But the pictures become simplified if we substitute a 1 in for the variables. Then the sides of the 30, 60, 90 triangle are 1, 2 and $\sqrt{3}$ and the sides of the 45, 45, 90 triangle are 1, 1 and $\sqrt{2}$. The variable just tells us that if we multiply one of these sides by a number, then we have to multiply the other two sides by the same number. For example, instead of 1, 1 and $\sqrt{2}$, we can have 3, 3 and $3\sqrt{2}$ (here $s = 3$), or $\sqrt{2}$, $\sqrt{2}$, and 2 (here $s = \sqrt{2}$).

* **Trigonometric solution:** The shorter leg of the triangle is adjacent to the 60° angle. So we will use cosine. We have $\cos 60° = \frac{ADJ}{HYP} = \frac{ADJ}{4}$. So ADJ = $4\cos 60° = 4(\frac{1}{2}) = 2$, choice (A).

Remarks: (1) If you do not see why we have $\cos 60° = \frac{ADJ}{HYP}$, review the basic trigonometry given after the solution to problem 9.

(2) To get from $\cos 60° = \frac{ADJ}{4}$ to ADJ = $4\cos 60°$, we simply multiply each side of the first equation by 4.

For those of you that like to cross multiply, the original equation can first be rewritten as $\frac{\cos 60°}{1} = \frac{ADJ}{4}$.

(3) There are several ways to compute $\cos 60°$. The easiest is to simply put it into your calculator (if you are allowed to use your calculator for the question). The output will be .5.

(4) If you are using your calculator, make sure it is in degree mode. Otherwise you will get an incorrect answer.

If you are using a TI-84 (or equivalent) calculator press MODE and on the third line make sure that DEGREE is highlighted. If it is not, scroll down and select it. If possible, do not alter this setting until you are finished taking your test.

(5) We can also compute $\cos 60°$ using the figure from the first solution (given on the SAT). For this problem, we have $\cos 60° = \frac{ADJ}{HYP} = \frac{x}{2x} = \frac{1}{2}$.

57. In ΔDOG, the measure of $\angle D$ is 60° and the measure of $\angle O$ is 30°. If $\overline{DO}$ is 8 units long, what is the area, in square units, of ΔDOG ?

   (A) 4
   (B) 8
   (C) $8\sqrt{2}$
   (D) $8\sqrt{3}$

* **Solution using a 30, 60, 90 right triangle:** Let's draw two pictures.

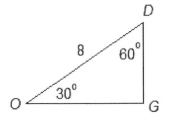
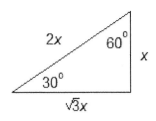

The picture on the left is what is given in the problem. Comparing this to the picture on the right we see that $x = 4$ and $\sqrt{3}x = 4\sqrt{3}$. So the area of the triangle is $\frac{1}{2}(4)(4\sqrt{3}) = 8\sqrt{3}$, choice (D).

Note: See problem 56 for more information on 30, 60, 90 triangles.

Trigonometric solution: We have $\sin 30° = \frac{DG}{8}$. So $DG = 8\sin 30°$. Similarly, $\cos 30° = \frac{OG}{8}$. So $OG = 8\cos 30°$. So the area of the triangle is $\frac{1}{2}(OG)(DG) = \frac{1}{2}(8\cos 30°)(8\sin 30°) = \frac{1}{2}\left(8 \cdot \frac{\sqrt{3}}{2}\right)\left(8 \cdot \frac{1}{2}\right) = 8\sqrt{3}$, choice (D).

Notes: (1) We can evaluate $\cos 30°$ and $\sin 30°$ by using the $30, 60, 90$ triangle shown in the figure above on the right.

$$\cos 30° = \frac{\text{ADJ}}{\text{HYP}} = \frac{\sqrt{3}x}{2x} = \frac{\sqrt{3}}{2} \quad \text{and} \quad \sin 30° = \frac{\text{OPP}}{\text{HYP}} = \frac{x}{2x} = \frac{1}{2}$$

(2) If we are allowed to use a calculator, then we can compute

$$\frac{1}{2}(OG)(DG) = \frac{1}{2}(8\cos 30°)(8\sin 30°) \approx 13.8564.$$

We can then plug the answer choices into the calculator to see that

$$8\sqrt{3} \approx 13.8564$$

So once again we get that the answer is choice (D).

Remark: Make sure that your calculator is in degree mode. Otherwise you will get the wrong answer (see problem 56).

58. In the (x, y) coordinate plane, what is the radius of the circle having the points $(2, -4)$ and $(-4, 4)$ as endpoints of a diameter?

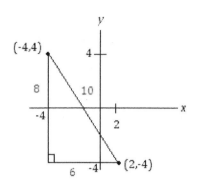

Solution using a right triangle: Let's plot the two points and form a right triangle.

We got the length of the left leg by subtracting 4 – (-4) = 4 + 4 = 8, and we got the bottom leg by subtracting 2 – (-4) = 2 + 4 = 6. We now use the Pythagorean Theorem:

$$c^2 = 6^2 + 8^2 = 36 + 64 = 100.$$

So $c = 10$.

It follows that the diameter of the circle is 10, and therefore the radius of the circle is **5.**

Remarks: (1) If you recognize that 6, 8, 10 is a multiple of the **Pythagorean triple** 3, 4, 5 (just multiply each number by 2), then you do not need to use the Pythagorean Theorem.

(2) 3, 4, 5 and 5, 12, 13 are the two most common Pythagorean triples.

(3) The radius of a circle is $\frac{1}{2}$ the diameter, or $r = \frac{1}{2}d$.

* Solution using the distance formula: We can find the length of the diameter of the circle by using the distance formula. We have

$$d = \sqrt{(-4-2)^2 + \left(4-(-4)\right)^2} = \sqrt{(-6)^2 + 8^2} = \sqrt{36 + 64} = \sqrt{100} = 10$$

It follows that the radius is $\frac{10}{2} = $ **5.**

Note: The distance between the two points (a,b) and (c,d) is given by

$$d = \sqrt{(c-a)^2 + (d-b)^2} \quad \text{or equivalently} \quad d^2 = (c-a)^2 + (d-b)^2$$

This formula is called the **distance formula**.

59.   ***** If $0 < x < 90°$ and $\sin x = 0.525$, what is the value of $\cos(\frac{x}{3})$

* Calculator solution:

$$x = \sin^{-1} 0.525 \approx 31.67. \text{ So } \cos(\frac{x}{3}) \approx \cos\left(\frac{31.67}{3}\right) \approx .983.$$

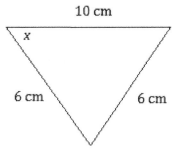

Note: Figure not drawn to scale.

60. The dimensions of a triangular block are shown above. What is the value of $\cos x$?

* Since the triangle is isosceles, the median and altitude from the vertex are the same.

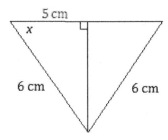

It follows that $\cos x = \dfrac{\text{ADJ}}{\text{HYP}} = \dfrac{5}{6}$ or **.833**.

Notes: (1) A triangle is **isosceles** if it has two sides of equal length. Equivalently, an isosceles triangle has two angles of equal measure.

(2) An **altitude** of a triangle is perpendicular to the base. A **median** of a triangle splits the base into two equal parts. An **angle bisector** of a triangle splits an angle into two equal parts. In an isosceles triangle, the altitude, median, and angle bisector are all equal (when you choose the base that is **not** one of the equal sides).

LEVEL 3: PASSPORT TO ADVANCED MATH

61. If $b = 5a^3 - 2a + 7$ and $c = 2a^2 + a + 3$, what is $3c - b$ in terms of a ?

(A) $-5a^3 + 6a^2 + a + 16$
(B) $-5a^3 + 6a^2 + 3a - 4$
(C) $-5a^3 + 6a^2 + 5a + 2$
(D) $a^2 + 5a + 2$

* Algebraic solution: $3c - b = 3(2a^2 + a + 3) - (5a^3 - 2a + 7)$
$$= 6a^2 + 3a + 9 - 5a^3 + 2a - 7 = -5a^3 + 6a^2 + 5a + 2.$$

This is choice (C).

Notes: (1) The distributive property needs to be used twice here. Make sure you are using it correctly.

The first time it needs to be used is when multiplying c by 3:

$$3c = 3(2a^2 + a + 3) = 6a^2 + 3a + 9.$$

A common mistake is to write $3(2a^2 + a + 3) = 6a^2 + a + 3$.

(2) An even more common error is to forget to put the expression for b in parentheses. This flawed computation would look like this:

$$3c - b = 3(2a^2 + a + 3) - 5a^3 - 2a + 7$$
$$= 6a^2 + 3a + 9 - 5a^3 - 2a + 7 = -5a^3 + 6a^2 + a + 16.$$

This error leads to choice (A), the wrong answer.

(3) Even when putting in the parentheses, many students mess this up. Look at the following use of the distributive property carefully:

$$-(5a^3 - 2a + 7) = -5a^3 + 2a - 7$$

(4) Negating an expression is equivalent to multiplying that expression by -1. This may help some students avoid the previous error.

More precisely, $-(5a^3 - 2a + 7)$ is the same as $-1(5a^3 - 2a + 7)$, so that $-(5a^3 - 2a + 7) = -1(5a^3 - 2a + 7) = -5a^3 + 2a - 7$.

Solution by picking a number: Let's choose a value for a, say $a = 2$. It follows that $b = 5a^3 - 2a + 7 = 5(2)^3 - 2(2) + 7 = 40 - 4 + 7 = 43$ and $c = 2a^2 + a + 3 = 2(2)^2 + 2 + 3 = 8 + 5 = 13$.

So $3c - b = 3 \cdot 13 - 43 = 39 - 43 = -4$.

Put a nice big, dark circle around the number -4 so you can find it easily later. We now substitute $a = 2$ into each answer choice:

(A) $-5a^3 + 6a^2 + a + 16 = -5(2)^3 + 6(2)^2 + 2 + 16 = 2$
(B) $-5a^3 + 6a^2 + 3a - 4 = -5(2)^3 + 6(2)^2 + 3 \cdot 2 - 4 = -14$
(C) $-5a^3 + 6a^2 + 5a + 2 = -5(2)^3 + 6(2)^2 + 5 \cdot 2 + 2 = -4$
(D) $a^2 + 5a + 2 = 2^2 + 5 \cdot 2 + 2 = 16$

Since choices (A), (B), and (D) did not come out correct, the answer is choice (C).

62. Jessica's car gets 18 miles per gallon when the car travels at an average speed of 35 miles per hour. Jessica begins a trip with 14 gallons of gas, and she travels at 35 miles per hour for the first 4 hours of her trip. Which of the following functions g is the most accurate model for the number of gallons of gas remaining in the tank t hours after the trip begins for $0 \le t \le 4$?

(A) $g(t) = \frac{14 - 35t}{18}$

(B) $g(t) = \frac{14 - 18t}{35}$

(C) $g(t) = 14 - \frac{35t}{18}$

(D) $g(t) = 14 - \frac{18}{35t}$

Solution by picking a number and estimation: Let's choose a value for t, say $t = 2$. In this case Jessica travels for 2 hours. Since she is travelling 35 miles per hour, she has travelled $d = rt = 35 \cdot 2 = 70$ miles. Since she gets 18 miles per gallon, she has used $\frac{70}{18} = \frac{35}{9} \approx 4$ gallons. So there is about $14 - 4 = \mathbf{10}$ gallons remaining in the tank.

Put a nice big, dark circle around the number 10 so you can find it easily later.

We now substitute $t = 2$ into each answer choice:

(A) $\frac{14 - 35 \cdot 2}{18} = \frac{-56}{18} < 0$

(B) $\frac{14 - 18 \cdot 2}{35} = \frac{-22}{35} < 0$

(C) $14 - \frac{35 \cdot 2}{18} = 14 - \frac{70}{18} \approx 14 - 4 = 10$

(D) $14 - \frac{18}{35 \cdot 2} = 14 - \frac{18}{70} > 13$

We see that the only possible answer is choice (C).

Notes: (1) Note that we picked a number that was simple but not too simple. The number 2 is usually a good choice if it is allowed.

(2) We used the formula "distance = rate × time" or $d = rt$.

In this problem the rate is $r = 35$ miles/hour and we chose $t = 2$ hours.

83

(3) Since $\frac{36}{9} = 4$, we have that $\frac{35}{9}$ is almost 4.

(4) Notice how we just estimated here. This worked out well because none of the answer choices wound up being close to each other with our chosen value for t. If two or more choices were close to 10, we would have needed to be more careful.

(5) If we are allowed to use a calculator for this problem, we would get a better decimal approximation for $\frac{70}{18}$ by dividing 70 by 18 in our calculator to get $14 - \frac{70}{18} \approx \mathbf{10.111}$

We could then also use our calculator for each answer choice. For example, $14 - \frac{35 \cdot 2}{18} \approx \mathbf{10.111}$.

(6) When using the strategy of picking numbers, it is very important that we check every answer choice. It is possible for more than one choice to come out to the correct answer. We would then need to pick a new number to try to eliminate all but one choice.

* Algebraic solution: When Jessica has travelled t hours, her total distance travelled is $d = rt = 35t$. Since she gets 18 miles per gallon, she has used $\frac{d}{18} = \frac{35t}{18}$ gallons, and therefore $14 - \frac{35t}{18}$ gallons of gas are remaining, choice (C).

Notes: (1) Notice how my algebraic solution mimics my solution of picking numbers.

(2) The algebraic solution is confusing without the specific numbers to guide you. Although picking numbers may take a little longer, in this case it is worth choosing that method over the algebraic method to avoid making a "careless" error.

63. What polynomial must be added to $x^2 + 3x - 5$ so that the sum is $5x^2 - 8$?

   (A) $4x^2 - 5x + 6$
   (B) $4x^2 - 3x - 3$
   (C) $5x^2 - 3x - 3$
   (D) $5x^2 + 3x + 6$

Solution by picking a number: Let's choose a value for x, say $x = 2$.

Then we have $x^2 + 3x - 5 = (2)^2 + 3(2) - 5 = 4 + 6 - 5 = 5$ and we also have $5x^2 - 8 = 5(2)^2 - 8 = 5(4) - 8 = 20 - 8 = 12$. So we must add **7** to get from 5 to 12 (indeed, $12 - 5 = 7$).

Put a nice big dark circle around **7** so you can find it easier later. We now substitute 2 for x into each answer choice:

(A) $4(2)^2 - 5(2) + 6 = 12$
(B) $4(2)^2 - 3(2) - 3 = 7$
(C) $5(2)^2 - 3(2) - 3 = 11$
(D) $5(2)^2 + 3(2) + 6 = 32$

Since (A), (C) and (D) each came out incorrect, the answer is choice (B).

Important note: (B) is **not** the correct answer simply because it is equal to 7. It is correct because all three of the other choices are **not** 7. **You absolutely must check all four choices!**

* Algebraic solution: We need to subtract $(5x^2 - 8) - (x^2 + 3x - 5)$. We first eliminate the parentheses by distributing the minus sign:

$$5x^2 - 8 - x^2 - 3x + 5$$

Finally, we combine like terms to get $4x^2 - 3x - 3$, choice (B).

Remark: Pay careful attention to the minus and plus signs in the solution above. In particular, make sure you are distributing correctly.

64. If -7 and 5 are both zeros of the polynomial $q(x)$, then a factor of $q(x)$ is

(A) $x^2 - 35$
(B) $x^2 + 35$
(C) $x^2 + 2x + 35$
(D) $x^2 + 2x - 35$

* Algebraic solution: $(x + 7)$ and $(x - 5)$ are both factors of $q(x)$. Therefore, so is $(x + 7)(x - 5) = x^2 + 2x - 35$, choice (D).

Note: There are several ways to multiply two binomials. One way familiar to many students is by FOILing. If you are comfortable with the method of FOILing you can use it here, but an even better way is to use the same algorithm that you already know for multiplication of whole numbers.

$$x + 7$$
$$\underline{x - 5}$$
$$-5x - 35$$
$$\underline{x^2 + 7x + 0}$$
$$x^2 + 2x - 35$$

What we did here is mimic the procedure for ordinary multiplication. We begin by multiplying -5 by 7 to get -35. We then multiply -5 by x to get $-5x$. This is where the first row under the first line comes from.

Next we put 0 in as a placeholder on the next line. We then multiply x by 7 to get $7x$. And then we multiply x by x to get x^2. This is where the second row under the first line comes from.

Now we add the two rows to get $x^2 + 2x - 35$.

Solution by plugging in answer choices: We are looking for the expression that gives 0 when we substitute in -7 and 5 for x.

Starting with choice (C) we have $5^2 + 2(5) + 35 = 70$. So we eliminate choice (C).

For choice (D) we have $5^2 + 2(5) - 35 = 0$ and $(-7)^2 + 2(-7) - 35 = 0$. So the answer is (D).

Notes: (1) c is a zero of a function $f(x)$ if $f(c) = 0$. For example, 5 is a zero of $x^2 + 2x - 35$ because $5^2 + 2(5) - 35 = 0$.

(2) A **polynomial** has the form $a_n x^n + a_{n-1} x^{n-1} + \cdots + a_1 x + a_0$ where $a_0, a_1, \ldots, a_n$ are real numbers. For example, $x^2 + 2x - 35$ is a polynomial.

(3) $p(c) = 0$ if and only if $x - c$ is a factor of the polynomial $p(x)$.

    65. What is the sum of the two solutions of the equation $x^2 - 7x + 3 = 0$?

* Quick solution: The sum of the solutions is the negative of the coefficient of the x term. So the answer is **7**.

Notes: (1) If r and s are the solutions of the quadratic equation $x^2 + bx + c = 0$, then $b = -(r + s)$ and $c = rs$. So in this problem the sum of the two solutions is 7 and the product of the two solutions is 3.

(2) Yes, you can also solve the equation $x^2 - 7x + 3 = 0$ by completing the square or using the quadratic formula, but this is very time consuming. It is much better to use the quick solution given above.

66. A function h is defined as follows:

$$\text{for } x > 0, h(x) = x^7 + 2x^5 - 12x^3 + 15x - 2$$
$$\text{for } x \le 0, h(x) = x^6 - 3x^4 + 2x^2 - 7x - 5$$

What is the value of $h(-1)$?

* Since $-1 \le 0$, we use the second equation. It follows that

$$h(-1) = (-1)^6 - 3(-1)^4 + 2(-1)^2 - 7(-1) - 5 = 1 - 3 + 2 + 7 - 5 = \textbf{2}.$$

LEVEL 3: PROBLEM SOLVING AND DATA

67. The mean length of a pop song released in the 1980's was 4 minutes and 8 seconds. The mean length of a pop song released in the 1990's was 4 minutes and 14 seconds. Which of the following must be true about the mean length of a pop song released between 1980 and 1999?

   (A) The mean length must be equal to 4 minutes and 11 seconds.
   (B) The mean length must be less than 4 minutes and 11 seconds.
   (C) The mean length must be greater than 4 minutes and 11 seconds.
   (D) The mean length must be between 4 minutes and 8 seconds and 4 minutes and 14 seconds.

Solution by picking numbers: Let's suppose that there are 2 pop songs from the 80's each with length 4 minutes and 8 seconds, and 4 pops songs from the 90's each with length 4 minutes and 14 seconds. Note that the given conditions are satisfied, and the combined mean is 4 minutes and 12 seconds. This eliminates choices (A) and (B).

Now let's reverse the situation, and suppose that there are 4 pop songs from the 80's each with length 4 minutes and 8 seconds, and 2 pops songs from the 90's each with length 4 minutes and 14 seconds. Note once again that the given conditions are satisfied, and the combined mean is 4 minutes and 10 seconds. This eliminates choice (C).

Since we have eliminated choices (A), (B), and (C), the answer is choice (D).

Notes: (1) The combined mean length would only be equal to 4 minutes and 11 seconds if the same exact number of pops songs were released in both the 80's and 90's.

(2) It is not true, of course, that there were only 2 pop songs released in the 80's and 4 pop songs released in the 90's. Nonetheless, we can use these simple numbers to eliminate answer choices.

(3) To actually compute the means above we use the formula

$$\text{Mean} = \frac{\text{Sum}}{\text{Number}}$$

where "Sum" is the sum of all the data, and "Number" is the amount of data. In each of the examples above there are 6 pieces of data so that the Number is 6.

(3) When computing the various means in the solution above, we need only worry about the seconds since the minutes are the same. For example, in the first paragraph, we can pretend that our data is 8, 8, 14, 14, 14, 14. The mean of this data is $\frac{8+8+14+14+14+14}{6} = \frac{72}{6} = 12$. It follows that the combined mean is 4 minutes and 12 seconds.

* **Direct solution:** Let's let a be the mean length of a pop song released in the 1980's, and b be the mean length of a pop song released in the 1990's. Since $a < b$, it follows that the combined mean m must satisfy $a < m < b$. That is, the combined mean must be between 4 minutes and 8 seconds and 4 minutes and 14 seconds.

68. Twenty-one people were playing a game. 1 person scored 50 points, 2 people scored 60 points, 3 people scored 70 points, 4 people scored 80 points, 5 people scored 90 points, and 6 people scored 100 points. Which of the following correctly shows the order of the median, mode and average (arithmetic mean) of the 21 scores?

(A) average < median < mode
(B) average < mode < median
(C) median < mode < average
(D) median < average < mode

* The **median** of 21 numbers is the 11th number when the numbers are listed in increasing order.

50, 60, 60, 70, 70, 70, 80, 80, 80, 80, **90**.

So we see that the median is 90.

The **mode** is the number that appears most frequently. This is clearly **100**.

Finally, we compute the **average**.

$$\frac{1 \cdot 50 + 2 \cdot 60 + 3 \cdot 70 + 4 \cdot 80 + 5 \cdot 90 + 6 \cdot 100}{21} \approx 83.33$$

Thus, we see that average < median < mode. This is choice (A).

69. The set Q consists of 15 numbers whose arithmetic mean is zero? Which of the following must also be zero?

   I. The median of the numbers in Q.
   II. The mode of the numbers in Q.
   III. The sum of the numbers in Q.

   (A) I only
   (B) II only
   (C) III only
   (D) I and III only

* **Solution by using a specific list:** Consider the following list:

$$-14, 1, 1, 1, 1, 1, 1, 1, 1, 1, 1, 1, 1, 1, 1$$

This list has an arithmetic mean of 0, but a median and mode of 1. So I and II do not need to be true. We can therefore eliminate choices (A), (B) and (D). So the answer is choice (C).

Note: To see that III must be true recall the formula

Sum = Average · Number

Since the average (arithmetic mean) is zero, so is the sum.

89

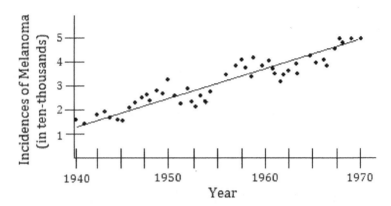

70. The scatterplot above shows the number of people diagnosed with melanoma, in ten-thousands, from 1940 to 1970. Based on the line of best fit to the data, as shown in the figure, which of the following values is closest to the average yearly increase in the number of incidences of melanoma?

    (A) 1,300
    (B) 330
    (C) 0.33
    (D) 0.13

* The average yearly increase in the number of incidences of melanoma is just the slope of the line of best fit. So we get approximately $\frac{50,000-10,000}{1970-1940} = \frac{40,000}{30} \approx 1,333.33$. So the best estimate is 1,300, choice (A).

Notes: (1) Remember that the slope of the line passing through the points (x_1, y_1) and (x_2, y_2) is $m = \frac{y_2-y_1}{x_2-x_1}$.

(2) In this problem we need to be a bit careful about the y-values. As an example, the number 1 on the y-axis actually represents 10,000 people, and not 1 person. So when we compute the slope we are using the points $(1940, 10,000)$ and $(1970, 50,000)$.

If we were to use the points $(1940, 1)$ and $(1970, 5)$ instead we would get a slope of $\frac{5-1}{1970-1940} = \frac{4}{30} \approx .13$, and we would choose (D), an answer choice which is <u>not</u> correct!

(3) As an alternative, we can use the points $(1940, 1)$ and $(1970, 5)$ to get a slope of approximately .13, and then multiply by 10,000 to get approximately 1,300, choice (A).

71. * John, a United States resident, is on vacation in Spain and uses his credit card to purchase a souvenir for 184 euros. The bank that issues the credit card converts the purchase price at the foreign exchange rate for that day, and an additional fee of 6% of the converted cost is applied before the bank posts the charge. If the bank posts a charge of $212 to John's account, what exchange rate, in Euros per one U.S. dollar, did the bank use?

* If we let C be the original cost of the item in dollars, then we have $C + .06C = 212$, or equivalently $1.06C = 212$. So $C = \frac{212}{1.06} = 200$.

So we know that 184 euros corresponds to 200 dollars. We want to know how many euros correspond to 1 dollar. So we set up a ratio.

The two things being compared are "euros" and "dollars."

euros	184	x
dollars	200	1

Now draw in the division symbols and equal sign, cross multiply and divide the corresponding ratio to find the unknown quantity x.

$$\frac{184}{200} = \frac{x}{1}$$
$$200x = 184 \cdot 1$$
$$x = \frac{184}{200} = .92$$

So we grid in **.92**.

72. Let a, b and c be numbers with $a < b < c$ such that the average of a and b is 2, the average of b and c is 4, and the average of a and c is 3. What is the average of a, b and c ?

* We change the averages to sums using the formula

$$\text{Sum} = \text{Average} \cdot \text{Number}$$

$$\text{So } a + b = 4$$
$$b + c = 8$$
$$a + c = 6$$

Adding these equations gives us $2a + 2b + 2c = 18$ so that $a + b + c = 9$. Finally, we divide by 3 to get that the average of a, b and c is $\frac{9}{3} = \mathbf{3}$.

LEVEL 4: HEART OF ALGEBRA

$$2x + y = 7 - 2y$$
$$5y - x = 5 - 4x$$

73. If (x, y) is a solution to the above system of equations, what is the value of $\frac{y+1}{x}$?

   (A) -11

   (B) $-\frac{1}{2}$

   (C) 2

   (D) 20

* Solution using the elimination method: We begin by making sure that the two equations are "lined up" properly. We do this by adding $2y$ to each side of the first equation, and adding $4x$ to each side of the second equation.

$$2x + 3y = 7$$
$$3x + 5y = 5$$

We will now multiply each side of the first equation by 5, and each side of the second equation by -3.

$$5(2x + 3y) = (7)(5)$$
$$-3(3x + 5y) = (5)(-3)$$

Do not forget to distribute correctly on the left. Add the two equations.

$$
\begin{array}{rl}
10x + 15y = & 35 \\
\underline{-9x - 15y = -15} & \\
x \qquad = & 20
\end{array}
$$

Using the first equation in the solution to find y, we have

$$2 \cdot 20 + 3y = 7$$
$$40 + 3y = 7$$
$$3y = 7 - 40 = -33$$
$$y = \frac{-33}{3} = -11$$

So $\frac{y+1}{x} = \frac{-11+1}{20} = -\frac{10}{20} = -\frac{1}{2}$, choice (B).

92

Remarks: (1) We chose to use 5 and −3 because multiplying by these numbers makes the y column "match up" so that when we add the two equations in the next step the y term vanishes. We could have also used −5 and 3.

(2) If we wanted to find y first instead of x we would multiply the two equations by 3 and −2 (or −3 and 2). In general, if you are only looking for one variable, try to eliminate the one you are **not** looking for. In this case we need to find both so it doesn't matter which we find first.

(3) We chose to multiply by a negative number so that we could add the equations instead of subtracting them. We could have also multiplied the first equation by 5, the second by 3, and subtracted the two equations, but a computational error is more likely to occur this way.

Solution using the substitution method: We solve the second equation for y and substitute into the first equation.

$5y = 5 - 3x$ implies $y = \frac{5-3x}{5} = \frac{5}{5} - \frac{3x}{5} = 1 - \frac{3x}{5}$. So now using the first equation we have

$$2x = 7 - 3y = 7 - 3(1 - \frac{3x}{5}) = 7 - 3 + \frac{9x}{5} = 4 + \frac{9x}{5}.$$

Multiply each side of this equation by 5 to get rid of the denominator on the right. So we have $10x = 20 + 9x$, and therefore $x = 20$.

Now proceed as in the previous solution to find $y = -11$, and so

$$\frac{y+1}{x} = \frac{-11+1}{20} = -\frac{10}{20} = -\frac{1}{2}, \text{ choice (B)}.$$

Remark: If we wanted to find y first instead of x we would solve the first equation for x and substitute into the second equation.

Solution using Gauss-Jordan reduction: As in the first solution (elimination method), we first make sure the two equations are "lined up" properly.

$$2x + 3y = 7$$
$$3x + 5y = 5$$

93

Begin by pushing the MATRIX button (which is 2ND x^{-1}). Scroll over to EDIT and then select [A] (or press 1). We will be inputting a 2×3 matrix, so press 2 ENTER 3 ENTER. We then begin entering the numbers 2, 3, and 7 for the first row, and 3, 5, and 5 for the second row. To do this we can simply type 2 ENTER 3 ENTER 7 ENTER 3 ENTER 5 ENTER 5 ENTER.

Note: What we have just done was create the **augmented matrix** for the system of equations. This is simply an array of numbers which contains the coefficients of the variables together with the right hand sides of the equations.

Now push the QUIT button (2ND MODE) to get a blank screen. Press MATRIX again. This time scroll over to MATH and select rref((or press B). Then press MATRIX again and select [A] (or press 1) and press ENTER.

Note: What we have just done is put the matrix into **reduced row echelon form**. In this form we can read off the solution to the original system of equations.

Warning: Be careful to use the rref(button (2 r's), and not the ref(button (which has only one r).

The display will show the following.

$$[\, [1 \ 0 \ 20]$$
$$[0 \ 1 - 11]]$$

The first line is interpreted as $x = 20$ and the second line as $y = -11$.

So we have

$$\frac{y+1}{x} = \frac{-11+1}{20} = -\frac{10}{20} = -\frac{1}{2}, \text{ choice (B)}.$$

Graphical solution: We begin by solving each equation for y.

$$3y = 7 - 2x \qquad\qquad 5y = 5 - 3x$$
$$y = \frac{7}{3} - \frac{2x}{3} \qquad\qquad y = 1 - \frac{3x}{5}$$

In your graphing calculator press the Y= button, and enter the following.

$$Y1 = 7/3 - 2X/3$$
$$Y2 = 1 - 3X/5$$

94

Now press ZOOM 6 to graph these two lines in a standard window. It looks like the point of intersection of the two lines is off to the right. So we will need to extend the viewing window. Press the WINDOW button, and change Xmax to 50 and Ymin to -20. Then press 2nd TRACE (which is CALC) 5 (or select INTERSECT). Then press ENTER 3 times. You will see that the point of intersection of the two lines is $(20, -11)$.

So $\frac{y+1}{x} = \frac{-11+1}{20} = -\frac{10}{20} = -\frac{1}{2}$, choice (B).

Remark: The choices made for Xmax and Ymin were just to try to ensure that the point of intersection would appear in the viewing window. Many other windows would work just as well.

74. If $y = 3^x$, which of the following expressions is equivalent to $9^x - 3^{x+2}$ for all positive integer values of x ?

 (A) $3y - 3$
 (B) $y^2 - y$
 (C) $y^2 - 3y$
 (D) $y^2 - 9y$

Solution by picking a number: Let's choose a value for x, say $x = 2$. Then

$$y = 3^2 = 9, \text{ and } 9^x - 3^{x+2} = 9^2 - 3^4 = 0.$$

Put a nice big dark circle around the number 0. We now substitute $y = 9$ into each answer choice.

 (A) $3 \cdot 9 - 3 = 27 - 3 = 24$
 (B) $9^2 - 9 = 81 - 9 = 72$
 (C) $9^2 - 3 \cdot 9 = 81 - 27 = 54$
 (D) $9^2 - 9 \cdot 9 = 81 - 81 = 0$

Since (A), (B) and (C) are incorrect we can eliminate them. Therefore, the answer is choice (D).

* Algebraic solution:

$$9^x - 3^{x+2} = (3^2)^x - 3^x 3^2 = (3^x)^2 - 9(3^x) = y^2 - 9y.$$

This is choice (D).

Note: For a review of the basic laws of exponents we used here see problem 50.

75. In the real numbers, what is the solution of the equation $4^{x+2} = 8^{2x-1}$?

(A) $-\dfrac{7}{4}$

(B) $-\dfrac{1}{4}$

(C) $\dfrac{5}{4}$

(D) $\dfrac{7}{4}$

* Algebraic solution: The numbers 4 and 8 have a common base of 2. In fact, $4 = 2^2$ and $8 = 2^3$. So we have $4^{x+2} = (2^2)^{x+2} = 2^{2x+4}$ and we have $8^{2x-1} = (2^3)^{2x-1} = 2^{6x-3}$. Thus, $2^{2x+4} = 2^{6x-3}$. So $2x + 4 = 6x - 3$. We subtract $2x$ from each side of this equation to get $4 = 4x - 3$. We now add 3 to each side of this last equation to get $7 = 4x$. Finally, we divide each side of this equation by 4 to get $\dfrac{7}{4} = x$, choice (D).

Notes: (1) For a review of the laws of exponents used here see the end of the solution to problem 50.

(2) This problem can also be solved by plugging in (start with choice C). We leave it to the reader to solve the problem this way. Make sure to use your calculator if you are allowed to.

76. If $i = \sqrt{-1}$, and $\dfrac{(7+5i)}{(-2-6i)} = a + bi$, where a and b are real numbers, then what is the value of $|a + b|$?

$$\ast \ \frac{(7+5i)}{(-2-6i)} = \frac{(7+5i)}{(-2-6i)} \cdot \frac{(-2+6i)}{(-2+6i)} = \frac{(-14-30)+(42-10)i}{4+36} = \frac{-44+32i}{40} = -\frac{44}{40} + \frac{32}{40}i$$

$$= -\frac{11}{10} + \frac{4}{5}i$$

So $a = -\dfrac{11}{10}$ and $b = \dfrac{4}{5}$.

Therefore $|a + b| = \left| -\dfrac{11}{10} + \dfrac{8}{10} \right| = \left| -\dfrac{3}{10} \right| = 3/10$ or $.3$.

Notes: (1) For a review of multiplying complex numbers see problem 26.

(2) The **conjugate** of $a + bi$ is $a - bi$. The product of conjugates is always a real number. In fact,

$$(a + bi)(a - bi) = a^2 + b^2$$

For example, $(-2 - 6i)(-2 + 6i) = (-2)^2 + 6^2 = 4 + 36 = 40$.

In practice, if you forget this rule, you can simply do the multiplication formally.

(3) One way to divide two complex numbers is to multiply both the numerator and denominator by the conjugate of the denominator. This is what was done in the first equality in the solution above.

Since the product of conjugates is always a real number, this method always produces a real number in the denominator. This allows us to write the quotient in the **standard form** $a + bi$.

    77. If $xy = 6, yz = 10, xz = 15$, and $x > 0$, then $xyz =$

Solution by trying a simple operation: The operation to use here is multiplication.

$$xy = 6$$
$$yz = 10$$
$$\underline{xz = 15}$$
$$(xy)(yz)(xz) = (6)(10)(15)$$
$$x^2y^2z^2 = 900$$

Notice that we multiply all three left hand sides together, and all three right hand sides together. Now just take the square root of each side of the equation to get $xyz = 30$. Thus, the answer is **30**.

* Quick computation: With a little practice, we can get the solution to this type of problem very quickly. Here, we multiply the three numbers together to get $(6)(10)(15) = 900$. We then take the square root of 900 to get **30**.

    78. If $5 - \frac{2}{x} = 2 - \frac{5}{x}$, then $\left|\frac{x}{3}\right| =$

* Algebraic solution: We add $\frac{5}{x}$ and subtract 5 from each side of the equation to get $\frac{3}{x} = -3$. We then take the reciprocal of each side to get $\frac{x}{3} = -\frac{1}{3}$. So $\left|\frac{x}{3}\right| = 1/3$ or **.333**.

LEVEL 4: GEOMETRY AND TRIG

79. If c is a positive constant different from $\frac{1}{2}$, which of the following could <u>not</u> describe the graph of $x + 2y = c(2x - y)$ in the xy-plane?

(A) A straight line passing through the origin that moves upwards from left to right
(B) A straight line passing through the origin that moves downwards from left to right
(C) The y-axis
(D) The x-axis

* **Quick algebraic solution:** Since c CANNOT be $\frac{1}{2}$, the given equation CANNOT be $x + 2y = \frac{1}{2}(2x - y)$.

Multiplying each side of this equation by 2 yields $2x + 4y = 2x - y$. We can cancel $2x$ from each side to get $4y = -y$, and then adding y to each side of this last equation gives $5y = 0$. Finally, dividing by 5 gives $y = \frac{0}{5} = 0$.

The equation $y = 0$ is precisely the x-axis, choice (D).

* **Alternate solution:** We solve the equation for y. Let's first distribute the c on the right hand side to get $x + 2y = 2cx - cy$. We now add cy to and subtract x from each side of the equation to get $2y + cy = 2cx - x$. Now factor y on the left and x on the right to get $(2 + c)y = (2c - 1)x$. Finally divide by $2 + c$ (assuming $c \neq -2$) to get $y = \frac{2c-1}{2+c}x$.

Note that this is a line passing through the origin. Since $c \neq \frac{1}{2}$, we have $2c - 1 \neq 2\left(\frac{1}{2}\right) - 1 = 1 - 1 = 0$. So the slope of the line cannot be 0, and therefore the line cannot be horizontal. Therefore, the graph cannot be the x-axis, choice (D).

Notes: (1) Note that the expression $\frac{2c-1}{2+c}$ is undefined when $c = -2$. Let's substitute $c = -2$ into the original equation:

$$x + 2y = (-2)(2x - y) = -4x + 2y$$

Subtracting $2y$ from each side of this equation gives $x = -4x$.

We now add $4x$ to each side of this last equation to get $5x = 0$.

Finally divide each side of this last equation by 5 to get $x = 0$. This is the y-axis.

This shows that the graph of the given equation CAN be the y-axis, and so we can eliminate choice (C).

(2) If $c > \frac{1}{2}$, then $2c - 1 > 2\left(\frac{1}{2}\right) - 1 = 1 - 1 = 0$, and $2 + c > 0$, and so $\frac{2c-1}{2+c} > 0$. In this case the slope of the line is positive, and so the graph will be a straight line passing through the origin that moves upwards from left to right. This eliminates choice (A).

(3) If $-2 < c < \frac{1}{2}$, then $2c - 1 < 2\left(\frac{1}{2}\right) - 1 = 1 - 1 = 0$, and $2 + c > 2 + (-2) = 0$, and so $\frac{2c-1}{2+c} < 0$. In this case the slope of the line is negative, and so the graph will be a straight line passing through the origin that moves downwards from left to right. This eliminates (B).

(4) I leave to the reader to determine what the graph of the given equation looks like when $c < -2$.

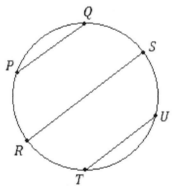

80. In the circle above with diameter d, chords $\overline{PQ}$ and $\overline{TU}$ are parallel to diameter $\overline{RS}$. If $\overline{PQ}$ and $\overline{TU}$ are each $\frac{3}{4}$ of the length of $\overline{RS}$, what is the distance between chords $\overline{PQ}$ and $\overline{TU}$ in terms of d?

   (A) $\frac{d\sqrt{7}}{8}$

   (B) $\frac{d\sqrt{7}}{4}$

   (C) $\frac{\pi d}{4}$

   (D) $\frac{3\pi d}{4}$

* Let's add some information to the picture.

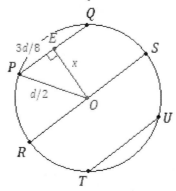

We draw segments $\overline{OP}$ and $\overline{OE}$ to form triangle OEP. Since the circle has diameter d, the radius of the circle is $\frac{d}{2}$. Note that $\overline{OP}$ is a radius of the circle and therefore has length $\frac{d}{2}$. Now we are given $PQ = \frac{3}{4}d$ so that $PE = \frac{1}{2}PQ = \frac{1}{2}\left(\frac{3}{4}d\right) = \frac{3d}{8}$.

We now use the Pythagorean Theorem to find x:

$$\left(\frac{d}{2}\right)^2 = x^2 + \left(\frac{3d}{8}\right)^2$$

$$\frac{d^2}{4} = x^2 + \frac{9d^2}{64}$$

$$x^2 = \frac{d^2}{4} - \frac{9d^2}{64} = \frac{16d^2}{16\cdot4} - \frac{9d^2}{64} = \frac{16d^2-9d^2}{64} = \frac{7d^2}{64}$$

So $OE = x = \frac{\sqrt{7}d}{8} = \frac{d\sqrt{7}}{8}$.

It follows that the distance between $\overline{PQ}$ and $\overline{TU}$ is $2OE = 2 \cdot \frac{d\sqrt{7}}{8} = \frac{d\sqrt{7}}{4}$, choice (B).

Notes: (1) In problems involving circles, it is often helpful to draw in your own radius. To find a suitable radius, look along the circumference of the circle for "key points." In the given figure, drawing a radius from the center of the circle to any of points P, Q, T, or U would work.

(2) The diameter of a circle is twice the radius, or $d = 2r$. Equivalently, the radius of a circle is half the diameter, or $r = \frac{d}{2}$.

(3) The Pythagorean Theorem says that if a right triangle has legs of length a and b, and a hypotenuse of length c, then $c^2 = a^2 + b^2$.

Note that the hypotenuse of a right triangle is always opposite the right angle, and the length of the hypotenuse is always by itself in the formula for the Pythagorean Theorem.

In this problem $a = x$, $b = \frac{3d}{8}$, and $c = \frac{d}{2}$.

(4) The distance between two parallel lines (or line segments) is the length of a line segment between the two lines that is perpendicular to both lines.

In this case, the distance between $\overline{PQ}$ and $\overline{TU}$ is $2OE$.

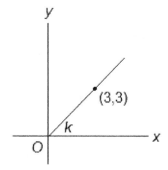

81. In the figure above, sin k = ?

   (A) $3\sqrt{2}$

   (B) $\frac{\sqrt{2}}{2}$

   (C) $\frac{\sqrt{3}}{2}$

   (D) 1

* Let's add a little information to the picture.

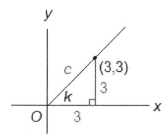

By the Pythagorean Theorem, $c^2 = 3^2 + 3^2 = 9 + 9 = 18$. So $c = \sqrt{18}$.

101

We have $\sqrt{18} = \sqrt{9 \cdot 2} = \sqrt{9}\sqrt{2} = 3\sqrt{2}$. So $c = 3\sqrt{2}$.

Now, $\sin k = \dfrac{\text{OPP}}{\text{HYP}} = \dfrac{3}{3\sqrt{2}} = \dfrac{1}{\sqrt{2}} = \dfrac{1}{\sqrt{2}} \cdot \dfrac{\sqrt{2}}{\sqrt{2}} = \dfrac{\sqrt{2}}{2}$, choice (B).

Remarks: (1) Since $18 = 9 \cdot 2$, $\sqrt{18}$ can be simplified as

$$\sqrt{18} = \sqrt{9 \cdot 2} = \sqrt{9}\sqrt{2} = 3\sqrt{2}. \text{ So } \dfrac{3}{\sqrt{18}} = \dfrac{3}{3\sqrt{2}} = \dfrac{1}{\sqrt{2}}.$$

Furthermore, we can rationalize the denominator in the expression $\dfrac{1}{\sqrt{2}}$ to get $\dfrac{1}{\sqrt{2}} \cdot \dfrac{\sqrt{2}}{\sqrt{2}} = \dfrac{\sqrt{2}}{2}$.

(2) Instead of using the Pythagorean Theorem, we can observe that the triangle we formed is an isosceles right triangle which is the same as a 45, 45, 90 right triangle. So the hypotenuse of the triangle has length $3\sqrt{2}$ (see the end of the solution to problem 56 for details).

(3) If we are allowed to use a calculator for this problem, then there is no need to simplify the square root or rationalize the denominator of the fraction. Once we get $c = \sqrt{18}$, we can use our calculator to get

$$\sin k = \dfrac{\text{OPP}}{\text{HYP}} = \dfrac{3}{\sqrt{18}} \approx .707.$$

We now use our calculator to approximate each answer choice, and we see that $\dfrac{\sqrt{2}}{2} \approx .707$. So the answer is choice (B).

82. Which of the following is equal to $\cos\left(\dfrac{\pi}{7}\right)$?

(A) $-\cos\left(-\dfrac{\pi}{7}\right)$

(B) $-\sin\left(\dfrac{\pi}{7}\right)$

(C) $\sin\left(\dfrac{5\pi}{14}\right)$

(D) $-\cos\left(\dfrac{5\pi}{14}\right)$

* **Solution using an identity:** We use the following cofunction identity:

$$\cos A = \sin\left(\dfrac{\pi}{2} - A\right)$$

So we have $\cos\left(\dfrac{\pi}{7}\right) = \sin\left(\dfrac{\pi}{2} - \dfrac{\pi}{7}\right) = \sin\left(\dfrac{5\pi}{14}\right)$, choice (C).

Notes: (1) A function f with the property that $f(-x) = f(x)$ for all x in the domain of f is called an **even** function.

$\cos x$ is an even function. It follows that $\cos(-A) = \cos A$. In particular, $\cos\left(-\frac{\pi}{7}\right) = \cos\left(\frac{\pi}{7}\right)$, and so $-\cos\left(-\frac{\pi}{7}\right) = -\cos\left(\frac{\pi}{7}\right) \neq \cos\left(\frac{\pi}{7}\right)$. This eliminates choice (A).

(2) $\cos A$ and $\sin A$ are *not* negatives of each other in general. If $\cos A = -\sin A$, then $\frac{\cos A}{\sin A} = -1$. Taking reciprocals, $\frac{\sin A}{\cos A} = -1$, so that $\tan A = -1$. This happens only when $A = \pm\frac{3\pi}{4}, \pm\frac{7\pi}{4}, \pm\frac{11\pi}{4}, \ldots$

This eliminates choice (B).

(3) Since we know that choice (C) is the answer, we can use the same reasoning as in note (2) to show that $\cos\left(\frac{\pi}{7}\right)$ cannot be equal to $-\cos\left(\frac{5\pi}{14}\right)$.

(4) If a calculator were allowed for this problem, we could simply approximate the given expression and all the answer choices in our calculator to get the answer.

Cofunction Identities:

$$\sin\left(\frac{\pi}{2} - A\right) = \cos A \qquad\qquad \csc\left(\frac{\pi}{2} - A\right) = \sec A$$

$$\cot\left(\frac{\pi}{2} - A\right) = \tan A$$

GET MORE PROBLEMS AND SOLUTIONS

Visit the following webpage and enter your email address to receive additional problems with solutions for free.

www.thesatmathprep.com/NewSAT2016.html

103

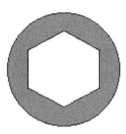

83. * The head of a copper "hexagon head screw bolt" (one cross section of which is shown above) has the shape of a cylinder with a hole shaped like a regular hexagon. The cylindrical head is 2 cm thick with a base diameter of 3 cm. The hexagonal hole is only half the thickness of the entire head, and each side of a hexagonal cross section has a length of 1 cm. Given that the density of copper is 8.96 grams per cubic cm, and density is mass divided by volume, find the mass of the head to the nearest gram.

* We first compute the volume of the head. There are two parts to the volume.

The bottom half of the head is a cylinder with height $\frac{2}{2} = 1$ cm and base radius $\frac{3}{2}$. It follows that the volume is $V = \pi r^2 h = \pi \left(\frac{3}{2}\right)^2 (1) = \frac{9\pi}{4}$ cm^3.

The top half of the head consists of the same cylinder as the bottom half, but this time we have to subtract off the volume of a hexagonal prism. The regular hexagonal face can be divided into 6 equilateral triangles, each with area $A = \frac{s^2\sqrt{3}}{4} = \frac{1^2\sqrt{3}}{4} = \frac{\sqrt{3}}{4}$. So the volume of the hexagonal prism is $V = Bh = \left(\frac{6\sqrt{3}}{4}\right)(1) = \frac{3\sqrt{3}}{2}$ cm^3 and the volume of the top half of the head is $\frac{9\pi}{4} - \frac{3\sqrt{3}}{2}$ cm^3

It follows that the total volume of the head is

$$\frac{9\pi}{4} + \left(\frac{9\pi}{4} - \frac{3\sqrt{3}}{2}\right) = \frac{18\pi}{4} - \frac{3\sqrt{3}}{2} = \frac{9\pi - 3\sqrt{3}}{2} \text{ cm}^3.$$

Finally, $D = \frac{M}{V} \Rightarrow 8.96 = \frac{M}{\frac{9\pi - 3\sqrt{3}}{2}} \Rightarrow M = 8.96 \cdot \frac{9\pi - 3\sqrt{3}}{2} \approx 103.39$ grams.

To the nearest gram, the answer is **103**.

Notes: (1) The radius of a circle is $\frac{1}{2}$ the diameter, or $r = \frac{1}{2}d$.

In this problem the base diameter of the cylinder is 3 cm. It follows that the base radius of the cylinder is $\frac{3}{2}$ cm or 1.5 cm.

(2) The volume of a cylinder is $V = \pi r^2 h$ where r is the base radius of the cylinder and h is the height of the cylinder.

For example, the bottom half of the screw is a cylinder with base radius $\frac{3}{2}$ cm and height 1 cm. So the volume is $V = \pi \left(\frac{3}{2}\right)^2 (1) = \frac{9\pi}{4}$ cm³.

(3) A **regular** polygon is a polygon with all sides equal in length, and all angles equal in measure.

The total number of degrees in the interior of an n-sided polygon is

$$(n - 2) \cdot 180$$

For example, a six-sided polygon (or **hexagon**) has

$$(6 - 2) \cdot 180 = 4 \cdot 180 = \mathbf{720} \text{ degrees}$$

in its interior. Therefore, each angle of a **regular** hexagon has

$$\frac{720}{6} = \mathbf{120} \text{ degrees.}$$

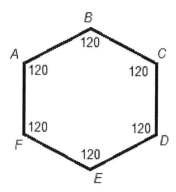

(4) For those of us that do not like to memorize formulas, there is a quick visual way to determine the total number of degrees in the interior of an n-sided polygon. Simply split the polygon up into triangles and quadrilaterals by drawing nonintersecting line segments between vertices. Then add 180 degrees for each triangle and 360 degrees for each quadrilateral. For example, here is one way to do it for a hexagon.

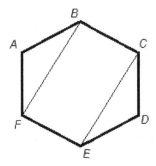

Since the hexagon has been split up into 2 triangles and 1 quadrilateral, the hexagon has 2(180) + 360 = **720** degrees. This is the same number we got from the formula.

To avoid potential mistakes, let me give a picture that would be incorrect.

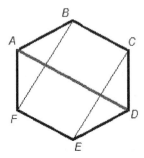

The above figure **cannot** be used to compute the number of interior angles in the hexagon because segment $\overline{AD}$ is "crossing through" segment $\overline{BF}$.

(5) Now let's draw a segment from the center of the hexagon to each vertex of the hexagon.

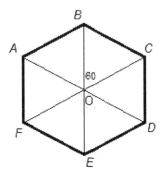

We see that the central angles formed must add up to 360 degrees. Therefore, each central angle is 60 degrees as shown in the figure above.

In general, the number of degrees in a central angle of an n-sided polygon is $\frac{360}{n}$.

(6) It is worth looking at a regular hexagon in a bit more detail.

Each of the segments drawn in the last figure in note (5) is a radius of the circumscribed circle of this hexagon, and therefore they are all congruent. This means that each triangle is isosceles, and so the measure of each of the other two angles of any of these triangles is $\frac{180-60}{2} = 60$. Therefore, each of these triangles is **equilateral**. This fact is worth committing to memory.

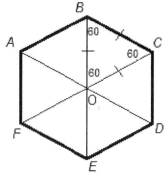

(7) The area of an equilateral triangle with side length s is $A = \frac{\sqrt{3}}{4}s^2$ (see note (8) below).

It follows that the area of an equilateral triangle with side length 1 is $\frac{\sqrt{3}}{4}(1)^2 = \frac{\sqrt{3}}{4}$.

(8) Most students do not know the formula for the area of an equilateral triangle, so here is a quick derivation.

Let's start by drawing a picture of an equilateral triangle with side length s, and draw an **altitude** from a vertex to the opposite base. Note that an altitude of an equilateral triangle is the same as the **median** and **angle bisector** (this is in fact true for any isosceles triangle).

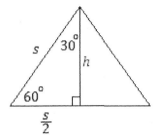

So we get two 30, 60, 90 right triangles with a leg of length $\frac{s}{2}$ and hypotenuse of length s.

We can find h by recalling that the side opposite the 60 degree angle has length $\sqrt{3}$ times the length of the side opposite the 30 degree angle. So $h = \frac{\sqrt{3}s}{2}$.

Alternatively, we can use the Pythagorean Theorem to find h:

$$h^2 = s^2 - \left(\frac{s}{2}\right)^2 = s^2 - \frac{s^2}{4} = \frac{3s^2}{4}. \text{ So } h = \frac{\sqrt{3}s}{2}.$$

It follows that the area of the triangle is

$$A = \frac{1}{2}\left(\frac{s}{2} + \frac{s}{2}\right)\left(\frac{\sqrt{3}s}{2}\right) = \frac{1}{2}s\left(\frac{\sqrt{3}s}{2}\right) = \frac{\sqrt{3}}{4}s^2.$$

(9) The volume of a prism is $V = Bh$ where B is the area of the base of the prism and h is the height of the prism.

In this problem we have a hexagonal prism with $B = \frac{6\sqrt{3}}{4} = \frac{3\sqrt{3}}{2}$ and $h = 1$. It follows that the volume of this prism is $V = \left(\frac{3\sqrt{3}}{2}\right)(1) = \frac{3\sqrt{3}}{2}$.

84.   * If $\cos x = 0.32$, then what is the value of $\sin x \tan x$?

* $x = \cos^{-1} 0.32$, and so

$$\sin x \tan x = \sin\left(\cos^{-1} 0.32\right) \tan\left(\cos^{-1} 0.32\right) \approx \textbf{2.81}.$$

LEVEL 4: PASSPORT TO ADVANCED MATH

$$\frac{1}{x} + \frac{3}{x} = \frac{1}{2}$$

85. Dennis is helping Billy assemble his new computer desk. Billy can put the desk together three times as fast as Dennis, and together Billy and Dennis can finish assembling the desk in 2 hours. The equation above represents this situation. Which of the following describes what the expression $\frac{3}{x}$ represents in this equation?

   (A) The fraction of the job that would be completed by Billy in 1 hour.
   (B) The fraction of the job that would be completed by Dennis in 1 hour.
   (C) The time, in hours, that it takes Billy to complete one third of the job.
   (D) The time, in hours that it takes Billy to assemble the desk by himself.

Solution by solving the equation: We can solve the given equation by first multiplying each side by $2x$ to get $2x \cdot \frac{1}{x} + 2x \cdot \frac{3}{x} = 2x \cdot \frac{1}{2}$, or equivalently $2 + 6 = x$. So $x = 8$. It follows that $\frac{3}{x} = \frac{3}{8}$.

It seems reasonable at this point that $\frac{3}{8}$ would represent the fraction of the job that Billy would complete in 1 hour.

Let's verify this. We assume that Billy can complete $\frac{3}{8}$ of the job in 1 hour. Since Billy can put the desk together three times as fast as Dennis, it follows that Dennis can complete $\frac{1}{8}$ of the job in 1 hour. So together they can complete $\frac{3}{8} + \frac{1}{8} = \frac{4}{8} = \frac{1}{2}$ the job in 1 hour, and therefore they can complete the whole job in 2 hours.

Since everything works out, the answer is choice (A).

Notes: (1) $\frac{1}{x}$ represents the fraction of the job that would be completed by Dennis in 1 hour. So Dennis can complete $\frac{1}{8}$ of the job in 1 hour.

(2) $\frac{1}{2}$ represents the fraction of the job that both Billy and Dennis, working together, can complete in 1 hour.

(3) The time it would take Dennis to complete the job himself is 8 hours.

(4) The time it would take Billy to complete the job himself is $\frac{8}{3}$ hours (or $2\frac{2}{3}$ hours).

* **Direct solution:** The right hand side of the equation, $\frac{1}{2}$, is the fraction of the job that both Billy and Dennis, working together, can complete in 1 hour.

On the left hand side of the equation we are expressing $\frac{1}{2}$ as a sum of two terms. Each term represents the portion of $\frac{1}{2}$ that each of Billy and Dennis contribute. Since Billy works three times as fast as Dennis, $\frac{3}{x}$ is the fraction of the job that Billy contributes, choice (A).

86. For all real numbers x, let the function g be defined by $g(x) = p(x - h)^2 + k$, where p, h, and k are constants with $p, k > 0$. Which of the following CANNOT be true?

   (A) $g(7) = -h$
   (B) $g(7) = 2$
   (C) $g(0) = -2$
   (D) $g(0) = 2$

Solution by plugging in answer choices: Let's start with choice (C) and suppose that $g(0) = -2$. We have $-2 = p(0 - h)^2 + k = ph^2 + k$. Since p and k are greater than 0, $ph^2 + k > 0$. Therefore $ph^2 + k$ CANNOT be -2, and the answer is choice (C).

Eliminating the other answer choices: This isn't necessary to solve the problem, but for completeness let's show that each of the other answer choices CAN be true.

(A) If $g(7) = -h$, then $-h = p(7 - h)^2 + k$. Let $h = -1$. Then $1 = 64p + k$, and so $k = 1 - 64p$. Now let $p = \frac{1}{128}$. Then $k = 1 - \frac{1}{2} = \frac{1}{2}$.

(B) If $g(7) = 2$, then $2 = p(7 - h)^2 + k$. Let $h = 0$. So $2 = 49p + k$, and therefore $k = 2 - 49p$. Now let $p = \frac{1}{49}$. Then $k = 2 - 1 = 1$.

110

(D) If $g(0) = 2$, then $2 = p(0 - h)^2 + k$. Let $h = 0$ and $p = 1$. Then $k = 2$.

87. On January 1, 2015, a family living on an island releases their two pet rabbits into the wild. Due to the short gestation period of rabbits, and the fact that the rabbits have no natural predators on this island, the rabbit population doubles each month. If P represents the rabbit population t years after January 1, 2015, then which of the following equations best models the rabbit population on this island over time?

    (A) $P = 2^{\frac{t+12}{12}}$
    (B) $P = 2^{t+1}$
    (C) $P = 2^{12t}$
    (D) $P = 2^{12t+1}$

Solution by picking a number: Let's choose a value for t, say $t = \frac{1}{2}$. Note that $\frac{1}{2}$ year is equal to 6 months.

Since there are initially 2 rabbits, after 1 month there are $2 \cdot 2 = 4$ rabbits, after 2 months there are $2 \cdot 4 = 8$ rabbits, after 3 months there are $2 \cdot 8 = 16$ rabbits, after 4 months there are $2 \cdot 16 = 32$ rabbits, after 5 months there are $2 \cdot 32 = 64$ rabbits, and after 6 months there are $2 \cdot 64 = $ **128** rabbits.

Put a nice big, dark circle around the number 128 so you can find it easily later.

We now substitute $t = \frac{1}{2}$ into each answer choice:

    (A) $2^{\frac{\frac{1}{2}+12}{12}} = 2^{\frac{\frac{1}{2}+\frac{24}{2}}{12}} = 2^{\frac{25}{2} \div 12} = 2^{\frac{25}{2} \cdot \frac{1}{12}} = 2^{\frac{25}{24}}$

    (B) $2^{\frac{1}{2}+1} = 2^{\frac{1}{2}+\frac{2}{2}} = 2^{\frac{3}{2}} = 8^{\frac{1}{2}} = \sqrt{8} = \sqrt{4}\sqrt{2} = 2\sqrt{2}$

    (C) $2^{12 \cdot \frac{1}{2}} = 2^6 = 64$

    (D) $2^{12 \cdot \frac{1}{2}+1} = 2^{6+1} = 2^7 = 128$

Since choices (A), (B), and (C) did not come out correct, the answer is choice (D).

Notes: (1) Note that we picked the number $\frac{1}{2}$ as opposed to an integer like 2. This is because an integer like 2 will force us to do 24 computations or recognize a pattern. The fraction minimizes the amount of computation and the amount of critical reasoning needed. An even smaller fraction like $\frac{1}{3}$ or $\frac{1}{4}$ would have saved even more time.

(2) Instead of multiplying by 2 repeatedly we could save time by finding a pattern as follows:

After 0 months there are $2 = 2^1$ rabbits.

After 1 month there are $2 \cdot 2 = 2^2$ rabbits.

After 2 months there are $2 \cdot 2^2 = 2^{1+2} = 2^3$ rabbits.

This should be enough to see the pattern. Can you see that After n months there are 2^{n+1} rabbits? In particular, after 6 months there are $2^7 = 128$ rabbits.

(3) There is no reason to continue evaluating answer choices once it is clear that the choice will not yield the correct answer. For example, for choice (A) it is not hard to see that $2^{\frac{\frac{1}{2}+12}{12}} = 2^{\frac{12.5}{12}}$ could not possibly be equal to 128.

(5) If we are allowed to use a calculator for this problem, we could use it to compute the answer choices quickly. For example, with $t = \frac{1}{2}$, choice (A) would give $2\wedge(\,(1\,/\,2 + 12)\,/\,12) \cong 2.0586$. Clearly this is incorrect and so we can eliminate it.

(6) When using the strategy of picking numbers, it is very important that you check every answer choice. It is possible for more than one choice to come out to the correct answer. You would then need to pick a new number to try to eliminate all but one choice.

* Solution using the exponential growth model formula: A quantity that continually doubles over a fixed time period can be modeled by the exponential function $P = c(2)^{\frac{t}{d}}$ where c is the quantity at time $t = 0$, and d is the doubling time in years. In this case, there are initially 2 rabbits, so that $c = 2$, and the doubling time is every month, or every $\frac{1}{12}$ year.

It follows that $P = 2(2)^{t \div \frac{1}{12}} = 2(2)^{12t} = 2^1 2^{12t} = 2^{1+12t} = 2^{12t+1}$, choice (D).

Note: See problem 50 for a review of the laws of exponents used here.

Solution using a general exponential function: A general exponential function has the form $P(t) = a \cdot b^{ct}$, where $a = P(0)$ is the initial amount and b is the exponential rate.

In this problem, $a = P(0) = 2$, and since the population is doubling, the exponential rate is also $b = 2$. So we have $P(t) = 2 \cdot 2^{ct}$.

We are also given that the population doubles each month, so that $P\left(\frac{1}{12}\right) = 4$. So we have $4 = 2 \cdot 2^{\frac{c}{12}} = 2^{1+\frac{c}{12}}$. So $2^2 = 2^{1+\frac{c}{12}}$, and therefore $1 + \frac{c}{12} = 2$. Subtracting 1 from each side of this equation yields $\frac{c}{12} = 2 - 1 = 1$, and so $c = 1 \cdot 12 = 12$.

So $P(t) = 2 \cdot 2^{12t} = 2^1 \cdot 2^{12t} = 2^{1+12t} = 2^{12t+1}$, choice (D).

$$g(x) = x^4 - kx^3 + 13x^2 - 12x + 4$$

88. The function g is defined above, and k is a constant. In the xy-plane, the graph of g intersects the y-axis at $(0,4)$ and intersects the x-axis at $(1,0)$ and $(2,0)$. What is the value of k?

* Solution by plugging in the given points: We use the point $(1,0)$ and substitute in 1 for x and 0 for $g(x)$ to get

$$0 = 1^4 - k \cdot 1^3 + 13 \cdot 1^2 - 12 \cdot 1 + 4 = 1 - k + 13 - 12 + 4 = 6 - k.$$

So $k = 6$.

Notes: (1) If a point is an intersection point of the graph of g and something else, then in particular, that point lies on the graph of g.

This means that we can substitute any of the given points into the equation for g to get a true statement.

(2) For example, let's look at the point $(0,4)$. If we substitute in $x = 0$ and $y = g(x) = 4$ in the given equation, we get

$$4 = 0^4 - k(0)^3 + 13(0)^2 - 12(0) + 4$$

or equivalently, $4 = 4$, a true statement.

Unfortunately using this particular point isn't particularly helpful since the resulting equation does not involve k.

(3) It is much more useful to use the point $(1,0)$ as we did in the above solution.

(4) We could also use the point $(2,0)$, although this will lead to a messier computation:

$$0 = 2^4 - k(2)^3 + 13(2)^2 - 12 \cdot 2 + 4$$

So

$$0 = 16 - 8k + 13 \cdot 4 - 24 + 4 = 16 - 8k + 52 - 24 + 4 = 48 - 8k$$

Adding $8k$ to each side of this last equation gives $8k = 48$. So we have $k = \frac{48}{8} = 6$, as in the original solution.

$$3x^2 + 2y^2 = 550$$
$$2x + 12y = 0$$

89. If (x, y) is a solution to the system of equations above, what is the value of y^2 ?

* Solution by substitution: We solve the second equation for x by first subtracting $12y$ from each side to get $2x = -12y$. We then divide each side of this last equation by 2 to get $x = -6y$.

Now we replace x by $-6y$ in the left hand side of the first equation to get

$$3x^2 + 2y^2 = 3(-6y)^2 + 2y^2 = 3(36y^2) + 2y^2$$

$$= 108y^2 + 2y^2 = 110y^2 \, .$$

So we have $110y^2 = 550$, and so $y^2 = \frac{550}{110} = 5$.

90. The graph of $g(x) = (3x - 9)(x - 1)$ is a parabola in the xy-plane. If the vertex of this parabola has coordinates (h, k), what is the value of $h - k$?

* Solution by using the x-intercepts of the graph: $g(x) = 0$ when $3x - 9 = 0$ and $x - 1 = 0$, or equivalently $x = \frac{9}{3} = 3$ and $x = 1$.

The x-coordinate of the vertex of the parabola is midway between these two x values, and so $h = \frac{3+1}{2} = \frac{4}{2} = 2$. It follows that

$$k = g(2) = (3 \cdot 2 - 9)(2 - 1) = (-3)(1) = -3.$$

So $h - k = 2 - (-3) = 2 + 3 = 5$.

114

Notes: (1) $x = 1$ and $x = 3$ are called **zeros**, **roots**, or **solutions** of the function g. These are the x-values at which $g(x) = 0$.

For example, $g(1) = (3 \cdot 1 - 9)(1 - 1) = (-6)(0) = 0$.

(2) If $x = c$ is a zero of a function g, then the point $(c, 0)$ is an x-intercept of the graph of g.

So in this example, the x-intercepts of the graph of g are $(1,0)$ and $(3,0)$.

(3) The x-coordinate of the **vertex** (or **turning point**) of a parabola is always midway between the x values of the two x-intercepts of the parabola (if they exist).

(4) Once we find the x-coordinate h of the vertex, we can find the y-coordinate k of the vertex by substituting h into the function g. That is, $k = g(h)$.

Solution by putting the quadratic function into standard form: We have $g(x) = (3x - 9)(x - 1) = 3x^2 - 12x + 9$

$$= 3(x^2 - 4x + 3) = 3(x - 2)^2 - 3 \text{ (details below)}.$$

From the final form of g we see that the vertex of the parabola is $(2, -3)$. So $h = 2$, $k = -3$, and therefore $h - k = 2 - (-3) = 2 + 3 = \mathbf{5}$.

Notes: (1) The **general form** for the equation of a parabola is

$$y = ax^2 + bx + c.$$

We can put the function $y = g(x)$ into general form by simply multiplying $(3x - 9)$ and $(x - 1)$ together to get

$$(3x - 9)(x - 1) = 3x^2 - 3x - 9x + 9 = 3x^2 - 12x + 9$$

This form however is not that useful for identifying specific information about the parabola such as the vertex.

(3) The **standard form** for the equation of a parabola is

$$y = a(x - h)^2 + k, \text{ or equivalently, } y - k = a(x - h)^2$$

In either of these forms, we can identify the vertex of the parabola as (h, k).

(4) To change an equation of a parabola from general form to standard form, we use a procedure called **completing the square**.

To complete the square on the expression $x^2 + bx$, we take half of the number b, and square the result to get b^2.

For example, to complete the square on $x^2 - 4x$, we half -4 to get -2, and then square -2 to get $(-2)^2 = 4$.

We then add this to the original expression to get $x^2 - 4x + 4$. This new expression is a perfect square. In fact, it factors as follows:

$$x^2 - 4x + 4 = (x - 2)(x - 2) = (x - 2)^2$$

Note that the number -2 is the same as the number we got from taking half of -4. This is not a coincidence. It always happens.

(5) We must have an expression of the form $x^2 + bx$ before completing the square. In other words, there *cannot* be a number in front of x^2 (in technical terms, the coefficient of x^2 must be 1).

In the given problem there is a coefficient of 3 in front of x^2. We deal with this by factoring 3 from the expression:

$$g(x) = 3x^2 - 12x + 9 = 3(x^2 - 4x + 3)$$

(6) Completing the square *does not* produce an expression that is equivalent to the original expression. For example, the expression $(x - 2)^2 = x^2 + 4x + 4$ is 4 more than the original expression $x^2 + 4x$.

We can fix this problem in two different ways:

Method 1: Add and subtract what we need inside the parentheses

Using this method, we write $g(x) = 3(x^2 - 4x + 4 - 4 + 3)$.

Notice how we added and subtracted 4 inside the parentheses.

We can now simplify this expression to

$$g(x) = 3(x^2 - 4x + 4 - 1) = 3(x^2 - 4x + 4) - 3 = 3(x - 2)^2 - 3$$

Note how we distributed the 3 to $(x^2 - 4x + 4)$ and (-1), a slightly unconventional use of the distributive property.

Method 2: Add what we need inside the parentheses and adjust the other constant accordingly.

Using this method, we write $g(x) = 3(x^2 - 4x + 4 - 1)$.

Since we added 4, we adjusted the 3 by subtracting 4, i.e. $3 - 4 = -1$.

Now proceed as in Method 1 to put the equation in standard form.

(7) If you don't like dealing with the 3 on the right hand side of the equation, it can temporarily be moved to the left before completing the square as follows:

We rewrite $g(x) = 3(x^2 - 4x + 3)$ as $\frac{g(x)}{3} = x^2 - 4x + 3$.

Now complete the square on $x^2 - 4x$ to get $x^2 - 4x + 4$. So we need to add 4 to the right hand side of the equation. We can undo this by either (i) subtracting 4 from the same side (as in Method 1 above), (ii) adjusting the 3 to -1 (as in Method 2 above), or (iii) adding 4 to the left hand side to balance the equation.

Let's use (iii) this time and write $\frac{g(x)}{3} = x^2 - 4x + 3$ as

$$\frac{g(x)}{3} + 4 = x^2 - 4x + 4 + 3$$

After completing the square we have $\frac{g(x)}{3} + 4 = (x - 2)^2 + 3$.

Subtracting 4 gives $\frac{g(x)}{3} = (x - 2)^2 - 1$.

Finally, multiplying by 3 yields $g(x) = 3(x - 2)^2 - 3$.

(8) Once the equation is in the standard form

$$g(x) = 3(x - 2)^2 - 3 \quad \text{or} \quad g(x) + 3 = 3(x - 2)^2$$

we can easily pick out the vertex by matching the equation up with the standard form

$$y = a(x - h)^2 + k \quad \text{or} \quad y - k = a(x - h)^2$$

Observe that $h = 2$ and $k = -3$.

(9) It is very common for students to make sign errors here. Note that the expression $(x - 2)^2$ indicates that $h = 2$, whereas the expression $g(x) + 3$ indicates that $k = -3$.

To see this, note that $g(x) + 3 = g(x) - (-3)$.

LEVEL 4: PROBLEM SOLVING AND DATA

$$S = 25.33H + 353.16$$

91. The linear regression model above is based on an analysis of the relationship between SAT math scores (S) and the number of hours spent studying for SAT math (H). Based on this model, which of the following statements must be true?

    I. The slope indicates that as H increases by 1, S decreases by 25.33.
    II. For a student that studies 15 hours for SAT math, the predicted SAT math score is greater than 700.
    III. There is a negative correlation between H and S.

    (A) I only
    (B) II only
    (C) III only
    (D) I and II only

* The slope of the line is $25.33 = \frac{25.33}{1}$. This indicates that as H increases by 1, S increases by 25.33. Also since the slope is positive, there is a **positive correlation** between H and S. So I and III are false, and the answer must be choice (B).

Notes: (1) We did not have to check II because once we determined that I and III were false, there was only one answer choice left that excluded both of them.

(2) For completeness let's check that II is true. To see this, we just need to perform the following computation:

$$25.33(15) + 353.16 = 733.11 > 700.$$

92. 2500 single men and 2500 single women were asked about whether they owned any dogs or cats. The table below displays a summary of the results.

	Dogs Only	Cats Only	Both	Neither	Total
Men	920	270	50	1260	2500
Women	750	430	340	980	2500
Total	1670	700	390	2240	5000

Of the people who said they had neither dogs nor cats, 200 were selected at random, and they were asked if they had any pets at all. 43 people said they did have pets, and the remaining 157 said that they did not. Based on both the initial data given in the table, together with the new data stated in this paragraph, which of the following is most likely to be accurate?

(A) Approximately 482 of the original people surveyed would say that they have no pets.

(B) Approximately 1758 of the original people surveyed would say that they have no pets.

(C) Approximately 1963 of the original people surveyed would say that they have no pets.

(D) Approximately 3925 of the original people surveyed would say that they have no pets.

* $\frac{157}{200} \cdot 2240 = 1758.4 \approx 1758$. So the answer is choice (B).

Notes: (1) We are being asked to extrapolate information from a random sample. In this case we want to estimate the number of people who have no pets at all. We can do this by multiplying the fraction of people in the random sample who have no pets by the total number of people with no cat or dogs.

(2) The fraction of people from the random sample with no pets is $\frac{157}{200}$.

(3) The total number of people with no cats or dogs is 2240, as can be seen from the table.

93. On a certain exam, the median grade for a group of 25 students is 67. If the highest grade on the exam is 90, which of the following could be the number of students that scored 67 on the exam?

> I. 5
> II. 20
> III. 24

> (A) I only
> (B) III only
> (C) I and II only
> (D) I, II, and III

* The highest exam grade must be 90. If the other 24 exam grades are 67, then the median will be 67. So III is possible.

If 5 of the exam grades are 90 and the remaining 20 are 67, then the median will be 67. So II is possible.

Finally, if 10 of the exam grades are 90, 10 are 60 and 5 are 67, then the median will be 67. So I is possible.

Therefore the answer is choice (D).

94. If the average (arithmetic mean) of k and $k + 7$ is b and if the average of k and $k - 11$ is c, what is the sum of b and c?

> (A) $2k - 2$
> (B) $2k - 1$
> (C) $2k$
> (D) $2k + \frac{1}{2}$

* **Solution by changing averages to sums:** Note that the sum of k and $k + 7$ is $k + (k + 7) = 2k + 7$, so that $2k + 7 = 2b$. Similarly, the sum of k and $k - 11$ is $k + (k - 11) = 2k - 11$ so that $2k - 11 = 2c$. So,

$$2b + 2c = 4k - 4$$
$$2(b + c) = 4k - 4$$
$$b + c = \frac{4k - 4}{2} = \frac{4k}{2} - \frac{4}{2} = 2k - 2$$

Thus, the answer is choice (A).

Solution by picking numbers: Let us choose a value for k, say $k = 5$. It follows that $k + 7 = 5 + 7 = 12$ and $k - 11 = 5 - 11 = -6$. So,

$$b = \frac{5 + 12}{2} = \frac{17}{2} = 8.5$$
$$c = \frac{5 - 6}{2} = -\frac{1}{2} = -0.5$$

and the sum of b and c is $b + c = 8.5 - 0.5 = \mathbf{8}$. Put a nice big, dark circle around this number so that you can find it easily later. We now substitute $k = 5$ into each answer choice.

(A) 8
(B) 9
(C) 10
(D) 10.5

Compare each of these numbers to the number that we put a nice big, dark circle around. Since (B), (C) and (D) are incorrect we can eliminate them. Therefore, the answer is choice (A).

Important note: (A) is **not** the correct answer simply because it is equal to 8. It is correct because all three of the other choices are **not** 8. **You** absolutely must check all four choices!

95. A farmer purchased several animals from a neighboring farmer: 6 animals costing \$100 each, 10 animals costing \$200 each, and k animals costing \$400 each, where k is a positive odd integer. If the median price for all the animals was \$200, what is the greatest possible value of k?

* **Solution by listing:** Let's list the prices in increasing order, including repetitions.

100, 100, 100, 100, 100, 100, 200, 200, 200, 200, 200, 200, 200, 200, 200, **200**, 400, …

In order for k to be as large as possible we need the 200 in bold to be the median. Since there are 15 numbers **before** the bold 200, we need 15 numbers **after** the bold 200 as well. So $k = \mathbf{15}$.

96. The average (arithmetic mean) salary of employees at an advertising firm with P employees in thousands of dollars is 53, and the average salary of employees at an advertising firm with Q employees in thousands of dollars is 95. When the salaries of both firms are combined, the average salary in thousands of dollars is 83. What is the value of $\frac{P}{Q}$?

121

* Solution by changing averages to sums: The Sum of the salaries of employees at firm P (in thousands) is $53P$.

The Sum of the salaries of employees at firm Q (in thousands) is $95Q$.

Adding these we get the Sum of the salaries of all employees (in thousands): $53P + 95Q$.

We can also get this sum directly from the problem.

$$83(P + Q) = 83P + 83Q.$$

So we have that $53P + 95Q = 83P + 83Q$.

We get P to one side of the equation by subtracting $53P$ from each side, and we get Q to the other side by subtracting $83Q$ from each side.

$$12Q = 30P$$

We can get $\frac{P}{Q}$ to one side by performing **cross division.** We do this just like cross multiplication, but we divide instead. Dividing each side of the equation by $30Q$ will do the trick (this way we get rid of Q on the left and 30 on the right).

$$\frac{P}{Q} = \frac{12}{30} = \frac{2}{5}$$

So we can grid in **2/5** or **.4.**

LEVEL 5: HEART OF ALGEBRA

97. If $x^{12} = \frac{3}{z}$ and $x^{11} = \frac{3y}{z}$ which of the following is an expression for x in terms of y?

(A) $3y$

(B) $2y$

(C) y

(D) $\frac{1}{y}$

* Solution by trying a simple operation: The operation to use here is division. We divide the left hand sides of each equation, and the right hand sides of each equation. First the left. Recall that when we divide expressions with the same base we need to subtract the exponents.

Therefore, we have $\frac{x^{12}}{x^{11}} = x^1 = x$. Now for the right. Recall that dividing is the same as multiplying by the reciprocal. So, $\frac{3}{z} \div \frac{3y}{z} = \frac{3}{z} \cdot \frac{z}{3y} = \frac{1}{y}$. Therefore, $x = \frac{1}{y}$ and the answer is choice (D).

Alternate Solution: Multiply each side of each equation by z to get

$$zx^{12} = 3$$
$$zx^{11} = 3y$$

Multiplying each side of the second equation by x yields

$$zx^{12} = 3xy$$

So we have $3xy = 3$ from which it follows that $xy = 1$, or equivalently $x = \frac{1}{y}$. Thus, the answer is choice (D).

$$3x - 7y = 12$$
$$kx + 21y = -35$$

98. For which of the following values of k will the system of equations above have no solution?

(A) 9
(B) 3
(C) −3
(D) −9

The system of equations

$$ax + by = c$$
$$dx + ey = f$$

has no solution if $\frac{a}{d} = \frac{b}{e} \neq \frac{c}{f}$. So we solve the equation $\frac{3}{k} = \frac{-7}{21}$. Cross multiplying yields $63 = -7k$ so that $k = \frac{63}{-7} = -9$, choice (D).

Note: In this problem $\frac{b}{e} \neq \frac{c}{f}$. Indeed, $\frac{-7}{21} \neq \frac{12}{-35}$. This guarantees that the system of equations has no solution instead of infinitely many solutions.

* Quick solution: We multiply −7 by −3 to get 21. So we have $k = (3)(-3) = -9$, choice (D).

The **general form of an equation of a line** is $ax + by = c$ where a, b and c are real numbers. If $b \neq 0$, then the slope of this line is $m = -\frac{a}{b}$. If $b = 0$, then the line is vertical and has no slope.

Let us consider 2 such equations.

$$ax + by = c$$
$$dx + ey = f$$

(1) If there is a number r such that $ra = d$, $rb = e$, and $rc = f$, then the two equations represent the **same line**. Equivalently, the two equations represent the same line if $\frac{a}{d} = \frac{b}{e} = \frac{c}{f}$. In this case the system of equations has **infinitely many solutions**.

(2) If there is a number r such that $ra = d$, $rb = e$, but $rc \neq f$, then the two equations represent **parallel** but distinct lines. Equivalently, the two equations represent parallel but distinct lines if $\frac{a}{d} = \frac{b}{e} \neq \frac{c}{f}$. In this case the system of equations has **no solution**.

(3) Otherwise the two lines intersect in a single point. In this case $\frac{a}{d} \neq \frac{b}{e}$, and the system of equations has a **unique solution**.

These three cases are illustrated in the figure below.

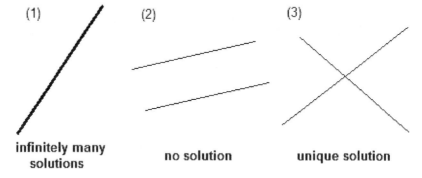

(1) infinitely many solutions

(2) no solution

(3) unique solution

Additional examples: The following two equations represent the same line.

$$2x + 8y = 6$$
$$3x + 12y = 9$$

To see this note that $\frac{2}{3} = \frac{8}{12} = \frac{6}{9}$ (or equivalently, let $r = \frac{3}{2}$ and note that $\left(\frac{3}{2}\right)(2) = 3$, $\left(\frac{3}{2}\right)(8) = 12$, and $\left(\frac{3}{2}\right)(6) = 9$).

The following two equations represent parallel but distinct lines.

$$2x + 8y = 6$$
$$3x + 12y = 10$$

124

This time $\frac{2}{3} = \frac{8}{12} \neq \frac{6}{10}$.

The following two equations represent a pair of intersecting lines.

$$2x + 8y = 6$$
$$3x + 10y = 9$$

This time $\frac{2}{3} \neq \frac{8}{10}$.

99. If $x + y = 2k - 1$, and $x^2 + y^2 = 9 - 4k + 2k^2$, what is xy in terms of k?

    (A) $k - 2$
    (B) $(k - 2)^2$
    (C) $(k + 2)^2$
    (D) $k^2 - 4$

Solution by picking numbers: Let $k = 0$. Then we have $x + y = -1$, and $x^2 + y^2 = 9$.

$$(x + y)^2 = (x + y)(x + y) = x^2 + 2xy + y^2 = x^2 + y^2 + 2xy.$$
$$(-1)^2 = 9 + 2xy$$
$$1 = 9 + 2xy$$
$$-8 = 2xy$$
$$-4 = xy$$

Put a nice big dark circle around the number **−4**. Now substitute $k = 0$ into each answer choice.

    (A) -2
    (B) 4
    (C) 4
    (D) -4

Since (A), (B) and (C) came out incorrect we can eliminate them, and the answer is choice (D).

* Algebraic solution:
$$(x + y)^2 = x^2 + y^2 + 2xy.$$
$$(2k - 1)^2 = 9 - 4k + 2k^2 + 2xy$$
$$4k^2 - 4k + 1 = 9 - 4k + 2k^2 + 2xy$$
$$2k^2 - 8 = 2xy$$
$$2(k^2 - 4) = 2xy$$
$$k^2 - 4 = xy$$

So $xy = k^2 - 4$, choice (D).

100. On the number line, the distance between the point whose coordinate is *s* and the point whose coordinate is *t* is greater than 500. Which of the following must be true?

$$\text{I. } |s| \cdot |t| > 500$$
$$\text{II. } |s - t| > 500$$
$$\text{III. } t - s > 500$$

(A) I only
(B) II only
(C) I and II only
(D) I, II, and III

* The first sentence is precisely the statement of II. Letting *s* = 1000 and *t* = 0 gives a counterexample for both I and III. The answer is choice (B).

$$k = a - b + 12$$
$$k = b - c - 17$$
$$k = c - a + 11$$

101. In the system of equations above, what is the value of *k* ?

* **Solution by trying a simple operation:** Notice that when we add the three given equations, all the variables on the right hand side add to zero. So we have $3k = 12 - 17 + 11 = 6$. Therefore $k = \frac{6}{3} = \mathbf{2}$.

102. An elephant traveled 7 miles at an average rate of 4 miles per hour and then traveled the next 7 miles at an average rate of 1 mile per hour. What was the average speed, in miles per hour, of the elephant for the 14 miles?

* **Solution using Xiggi's formula:**

$$\text{Average Speed} = \frac{2(4)(1)}{4 + 1} = \textbf{8/5 or 1.6}$$

Note: The following simple formula can be used to find an average speed when two individual speeds for the same distance are known.

$$\textbf{Average Speed} = \frac{\textbf{2(Speed 1)(Speed 2)}}{\textbf{Speed 1 + Speed 2}}$$

I call the above formula **Xiggi's formula** (it is more commonly known as the **Harmonic Mean formula**).

126

Solution using a "distance = rate · time chart": Let's put the given information into the following chart:

	Distance	Rate	Time
1st part of trip	7	4	$\frac{7}{4}$
2nd part of trip	7	1	$\frac{7}{1} = 7$
total	14		8.75

Note that we computed the times by using "distance = rate · time" in the form "time $= \frac{\text{distance}}{\text{rate}}$." Finally, we use the formula in the form

$$\text{rate} = \frac{\text{distance}}{\text{time}} = \frac{14}{8.75} = \mathbf{1.6}.$$

Note: To get the total distance we add the two distances, and to get the total time we add the two times. Be careful – this doesn't work for rates!

LEVEL 5: GEOMETRY AND TRIG

103. If $0 \leq x \leq 360°$, $\tan x < 0$ and $\cos x \tan x > 0$, then which of the following is a possible value for x ?

  (A) 30°
  (B) 150°
  (C) 210°
  (D) 330°

* $\tan x < 0$ in Quadrants II and IV. Since $\cos x \tan x > 0$ we must have $\cos x < 0$. This is true in Quadrants II and III. So x must be in Quadrant II and therefore $90° < x < 180°$. So the answer is choice (B).

Note: Many students find it helpful to remember the following diagram.

127

This diagram tells us which trig functions are positive in which quadrants. The **A** stands for "all" so that all trig functions are positive in the first quadrant. Similarly, **S** stands for "sine," **T** stands for "tangent," and **C** stands for "cosine."

So, for example, if angle x is in the second quadrant, then $\sin x > 0$, $\tan x < 0$ and $\cos x < 0$.

104. For $0 < x < 90°$,

$$\tan x - \tan(-x) + \sin x - \sin(-x) + \cos x - \cos(-x) =$$

    (A) 0
    (B) 3
    (C) $2 \tan x$
    (D) $2 \tan x + 2 \sin x$

* $\cos x$ is an even function, so that $\cos(-x) = \cos x$. Also, $\sin x$ and $\tan x$ are odd functions, so $\sin(-x) = -\sin x$ and $\tan(-x) = -\tan x$. So we get

$$\tan x - \tan(-x) + \sin x - \sin(-x) + \cos x - \cos(-x)$$
$$= \tan x + \tan x + \sin x + \sin x + \cos x - \cos x$$
$$= 2 \tan x + 2 \sin x$$

This is choice (D).

Negative Identities: These identities are just restating what was already described above.

$$\cos(-A) = \cos A \qquad\qquad \sin(-A) = -\sin A$$
$$\tan(-A) = -\tan A$$

105. It is given that $\cos x = k$, where x is the radian measure of an angle and $\pi < x < \frac{3\pi}{2}$. If $\cos z = -k$, which of the following could <u>not</u> be the value of z ?

    (A) $x - \pi$
    (B) $\pi - x$
    (C) $2\pi - x$
    (D) $3\pi - x$

* **Solution using coterminal angles and a negative identity:**

$$\cos(2\pi - x) = \cos(x - 2\pi) = \cos x = k \neq -k.$$

128

So $2\pi - x$ could not be the value of z, choice (C).

Notes: (1) For the first equality we used the negative identity

$$\cos(-A) = \cos A$$

(see problem 104), together with the fact that $x - 2\pi = -(2\pi - x)$.

(2) In general we have $a - b = -(b - a)$. To see this simply distribute:

$$-(b - a) = -b + a = a - b.$$

(3) Using notes (1) and (2) together, we have

$$\cos(2\pi - x) = \cos(-(x - 2\pi)) = \cos(x - 2\pi).$$

(4) For the second equality we used the fact that x and $x - 2\pi$ are **coterminal angles**.

If a and b are coterminal angles, then $\cos a = \cos b$.

(5) Given an angle x, we get a coterminal angle by adding or subtracting any integer multiple of 2π. So the following are all coterminal with x:

$$... x - 4\pi, x - 2\pi, x, x + 2\pi, x + 4\pi, ...$$

Solution using the cosine difference identity:

$$\mathbf{\cos(A - B) = \cos A \, \cos B + \sin A \, \sin B}$$

Let's start with choice (C), and apply the difference identity:

$$\cos(2\pi - x) = \cos 2\pi \, \cos x + \sin 2\pi \, \sin x$$

$$= 1 \cdot \cos x + 0 \cdot \sin x = \cos x = k \neq -k.$$

So $2\pi - x$ could not be the value of z, choice (C).

Notes: (1) Choice (C) is always a good choice to start with when plugging in.

(2) Let's apply the difference formula to the other answer choices as well:

$$\cos(x - \pi) = \cos x \, \cos \pi + \sin x \, \sin \pi$$

$$= \cos x \, (-1) + \sin x \, (0) = - \cos x = -k.$$

This shows that z can be $x - \pi$, and so we can eliminate choice (A).

For $\pi - x$, we can use the difference identity again, or we can use the negative identity as we did in the last solution to get

$$\cos(\pi - x) = \cos(x - \pi) = -k$$

This shows that z can also be $\pi - x$, and so we can eliminate choice (B).

$$\cos(3\pi - x) = \cos 3\pi \, \cos x + \sin 3\pi \, \sin x$$

$$= (-1)\cos x + 0 \cdot \sin x = -\cos x = -k.$$

This shows that z can also be $3\pi - x$, and we can eliminate choice (D).

(3) $3\pi = \pi + 2\pi$, and so π and 3π are coterminal angles. It follows that $\cos 3\pi = \cos \pi = -1$ and $\sin 3\pi = \sin \pi = 0$.

Solution using the unit circle: Since $\pi < x < \frac{3\pi}{2}$, when x is placed in standard position, its terminal side falls in the third quadrant, and $\cos x$ will be the x-coordinate of the point where the terminal side intersects the unit circle.

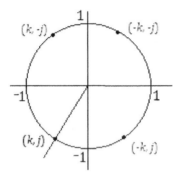

Since x is a third quadrant angle, it's reference angle is the first quadrant angle $x - \pi$, and so from the figure above we see that $\cos(x - \pi) = -k$.

The corresponding second quadrant angle is then $\pi - (x - \pi) = 2\pi - x$, and so we see from the figure that $\cos(2\pi - x) = k \neq -k$, and so z cannot equal $2\pi - k$, choice (C).

Notes: (1) If θ is a first quadrant angle, then the corresponding angle in the second quadrant is $\pi - \theta$.

The corresponding angle in the third quadrant is $\pi + \theta$.

And the corresponding angle in the fourth quadrant is $2\pi - \theta$.

So in this problem, the first quadrant angle is $x - \pi$, the corresponding second quadrant angle is $\pi - (x - \pi) = \pi - x + \pi = 2\pi - x$, the corresponding third quadrant angle is $(x - \pi) + \pi = x$, and the fourth quadrant angle is $2\pi - (x - \pi) = 2\pi - x + \pi = 3\pi - x$.

(2) From the last note, and the picture above we have $\cos(x - \pi) = -k$, $\cos(2\pi - x) = k$, $\cos x = k$, and $\cos(3\pi - x) = -k$.

$$x^2 + y^2 + 4x - 10y - 20 = 0$$

106. The graph of the equation above is a circle with center (h, k) and radius r. Compute $r \cdot (k - h)$.

* Solution by completing the square: Let's first rewrite the given equation as follows:

$$(x^2 + 4x) + (y^2 - 10y) = 20$$

Note that we regrouped the terms so that all terms involving x are together, all terms involving y are together, and the constant has been moved to the right hand side.

We now take half of 4 which is 2, and square this number to get 4.

We also take half of -10 which is -5, and square this number to get 25.

We add each of these numbers to both sides of the equation, grouping accordingly.

$$(x^2 + 4x + 4) + (y^2 - 10y + 25) = 20 + 4 + 25$$

We now factor each of the expressions in parentheses on the left hand side, and simplify on the right hand side.

$$(x + 2)^2 + (y - 5)^2 = 49$$

We see that $h = -2$, $k = 5$, and $r = 7$.

So $r \cdot (k - h) = 7\big(5 - (-2)\big) = 7 \cdot 7 = \mathbf{49}$.

Notes: (1) The given equation has a graph which is a circle, a point, or empty. On the SAT it will most likely be a circle.

(2) The **general form** for the equation of a circle is

$$x^2 + Bx + y^2 + Cy + D = 0.$$

This form is not that useful for identifying specific information about the circle such as its center and radius.

(3) The **standard form** for the equation of a circle is

$$(x - h)^2 + (y - k)^2 = r^2$$

In this form, we can identify the center as (h, k) and the radius as r.

(4) To change an equation of a circle from general form to standard form, we use a procedure called **completing the square**.

To complete the square on the expression $x^2 + bx$, we take half of the number b, and square the result to get b^2.

For example, to complete the square on $x^2 + 4x$, we half 4 to get 2, and then square 2 to get $2^2 = 4$.

We then add this to the original expression to get $x^2 + 4x + 4$. This new expression is a perfect square. In fact, it factors as follows:

$$x^2 + 4x + 4 = (x + 2)(x + 2) = (x + 2)^2$$

Note that the number 2 is the same as the number we got from taking half of 4. This is not a coincidence. It always happens.

When we complete the square on $y^2 - 10y$, we half -10 to get -5, and then square -5 to get $(-5)^2 = (-5)(-5) = 25$.

We then add this to the original expression to get $y^2 - 10y + 25$. This new expression is also a perfect square. In fact, it factors as follows:

$$y^2 - 10y + 25 = (y - 5)(y - 5) = (y - 5)^2$$

Notice again the number -5 appearing in this final expression.

(5) Completing the square *does not* produce an expression that is equivalent to the original expression. For example, the expression $(x + 2)^2 = x^2 + 4x + 4$ is 4 more than the original expression $x^2 + 4x$.

We fix this problem by adding the same quantity (in this case 4) to the other side of the equation.

(6) Once the equation is in the standard form

$$(x + 2)^2 + (y - 5)^2 = 49$$

we can easily pick out the center and radius by matching the equation up with the standard form

$$(x - h)^2 + (y - k)^2 = r^2.$$

Observe that $h = -2$, $k = 5$, and $r = 7$.

(7) It is very common for students to make sign errors here. Note that the expression $(y - 5)^2$ indicates that $k = 5$, whereas the expression $(x + 2)^2$ indicates that $h = -2$.

To see this, note that $(x + 2)^2 = \left(x - (-2)\right)^2$.

(8) Another common mistake is to say that $r = 49$. This is not true. $r^2 = 49$, so that $r = 7$.

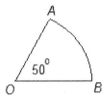

107. * In the figure above, AB is the arc of a circle with center O. If the length of arc AB is 4π, what is the area of region OAB to the nearest tenth?

* We first find the circumference of the circle using the ratio $\dfrac{50}{360} = \dfrac{4\pi}{C}$.

Cross multiplying gives $50C = 1440\pi$, so $C = \dfrac{1440\pi}{50} = \dfrac{144\pi}{5}$.

Since $C = 2\pi r$, we have $2\pi r = \dfrac{144\pi}{5}$, so $r = \dfrac{72}{5}$.

The area of the circle is $A = \pi r^2 = \dfrac{5184\pi}{25}$.

Now we find the area of the sector using the ratio $\dfrac{50}{360} = \dfrac{a}{(5184\pi)/25}$.

Cross multiplying gives us $360a = 10{,}368\pi$.

So $a = \dfrac{10{,}368\pi}{360} \approx 90.478$. To the nearest tenth this is **90.5**.

Notes: Consider the circle in the following figure:

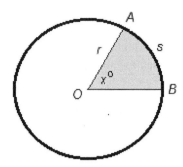

(1) Notice that $\overline{OA}$ and $\overline{OB}$ are both radii of the circle. So $OA = OB = r$. If we know the radius r, then we can find the diameter d of the circle, the circumference C of the circle, and the area A of the circle. Indeed, $d = 2r, C = 2\pi r$, and $A = \pi r^2$.

In fact, if we know any one of the four quantities we can find the other three. For example, if we know that the area of a circle is $A = 9\pi$, then it follows that $r = 3, d = 6$, and $C = 6\pi$.

(2) Suppose that in addition to the radius r, we know the angle x. We can then use the following ratio to find the length s of arc AB.

$$\frac{x}{360} = \frac{s}{C}$$

For example, if we are given that $r = 5$ and $x = 45$, then we have

$$\frac{45}{360} = \frac{s}{10\pi}$$

So $360s = 450\pi$, and therefore $s = \frac{450\pi}{360} = \frac{5\pi}{4}$.

In this particular example we can use a little shortcut. Just note that a 45 degree angle gives $\frac{1}{8}$ of the total degree measure of the circle, and therefore the arc length is $\frac{1}{8}$ of the circumference. So $s = \frac{10\pi}{8} = \frac{5\pi}{4}$.

(3) We can also use the following ratio to find the area a of sector AOB.

$$\frac{x}{360} = \frac{a}{A}$$

For example, if again we are given that $r = 5$ and $x = 45$, then we have

$$\frac{45}{360} = \frac{a}{25\pi}$$

So $360a = 1125\pi$, and therefore $a = \frac{1125\pi}{360} = \frac{25\pi}{8}$.

Again, we can take a shortcut in this example and just divide the area of the circle by 8 to get $a = \frac{25\pi}{8}$.

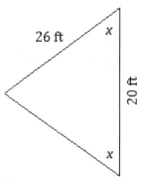

Note: Figure not drawn to scale.

108. * A homeowner drew a sketch of their triangle-shaped garden as shown above. Although the sketch was not drawn accurately to scale, the triangle was labelled with the proper dimensions. What is the value of $\sin x$?

* Since two of the angles of the triangle have equal measure, the triangle is isosceles. It follows that the median and altitude from the vertex of the triangle are the same.

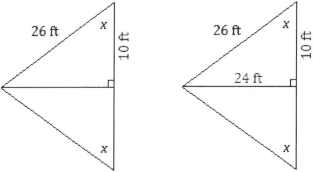

In the figure on the left we drew the altitude from the vertex angle. Since this is also the median, we get a right triangle with a leg of length $\frac{20}{2} = 10$ ft.

135

We can now find the length of the other leg by using the Pythagorean Theorem, or better yet, by noticing that we have a multiple of the Pythagorean triple 5, 12, 13. Since $10 = 5 \cdot 2$ and $26 = 13 \cdot 2$, it follows that the length of the other leg is $12 \cdot 2 = 24$ ft.

Finally, we have $\sin x = \dfrac{\text{OPP}}{\text{HYP}} = \dfrac{24}{26} = \dfrac{12}{13} \approx .923$

Note: See problem 60 for more information on medians and altitudes in isosceles triangles.

LEVEL 5: PASSPORT TO ADVANCED MATH

109. If the expression $\dfrac{9x^2}{3x+5}$ is written in the equivalent form $\dfrac{25}{3x+5} + k$, what is k in terms of x ?

     (A) $9x^2$
     (B) $9x^2 + 5$
     (C) $3x - 5$
     (D) $3x + 5$

* **Quick algebraic solution:** We have $\dfrac{9x^2}{3x+5} = \dfrac{25}{3x+5} + k$, so that

$$k = \dfrac{9x^2}{3x+5} - \dfrac{25}{3x+5} = \dfrac{9x^2-25}{3x+5} = \dfrac{(3x+5)(3x-5)}{3x+5} = 3x - 5, \text{ choice (C)}.$$

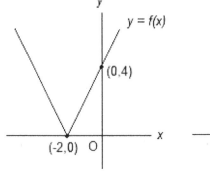
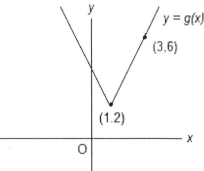

110. The figures above show the graphs of the functions f and g. The function f is defined by $f(x) = 2|x + 2|$ and the function g is defined by $g(x) = f(x + h) + k$, where h and k are constants. What is the value of $|h - k|$?

* Notice that to get the graph of g we shift the graph of f 3 units to the right, and 2 units up. Therefore $g(x) = f(x - 3) + 2$. So $h = -3$ and $k = 2$. Therefore $|h - k| = |-3 - 2| = |-5| = 5$.

Notes: (1) To translate the graph of a function up 2 units we add 2 to the original function.

(2) To translate the graph of a function right 3 units we replace x by $x - 3$ in the original function.

Review of basic transformations: Let $y = f(x)$, and $k > 0$. We can move the graph of f around by applying the following basic transformations.

$y = f(x) + k$ shift up k units
$y = f(x) - k$ shift down k units
$y = f(x - k)$ shift right k units
$y = f(x + k)$ shift left k units
$y = -f(x)$ reflect in x-axis
$y = f(-x)$ reflect in y-axis.

111. Let the function q be defined by $q(x) = a(x - h)^2$, where h is a positive constant, and a is a negative constant. For what value of x will the function q have its maximum value?

    (A) $-h$
    (B) $-a$
    (C) a
    (D) h

Solution by picking numbers: Let's substitute $h = 1$ and $a = -1$, so that $q(x) = -(x - 1)^2$. If we put this in our graphing calculator we see that the maximum occurs when $x = 1$. Substituting our chosen values for h and a into each answer choice yields

    (A) -1
    (B) 1
    (C) -1
    (D) 1

We can therefore eliminate choices (A) and (C). Let's try changing h to 2, and leaving $a = -1$, so that $q(x) = -(x - 2)^2$. Again checking this in our graphing calculator we get $x = 2$. Substituting the new values for h and a into answer choices (B) and (D) yields

(B) 1

(D) 2

Choice (B) does not give the correct answer this time so we can eliminate it. Thus, the answer is choice (D).

Remark: If we were a bit more careful about how we picked our original numbers we could have avoided having to do it twice. It is actually easy to see that choosing $h = 1$ and $a = -1$ will make some of the answer choices come out to the same number.

Finding the maximum without a graphing calculator: Let's use our second guess (since it turned out to be better).

Method 1: The **standard form** for a quadratic equation is

$$y - k = a(x - h)^2 \quad \text{or equivalently} \quad y = a(x - h)^2 + k$$

The graph is a parabola with vertex at (h, k). The parabola opens upwards if $a > 0$, and downwards if $a < 0$.

$q(x) = -(x - 2)^2$ is the standard form for a quadratic function whose graph is a parabola that opens downwards and has vertex $(2, 0)$. Thus the maximum occurs at $x = 2$.

Note: In this problem, $h = 2$ and $k = 0$. We substituted these values into the standard form for a quadratic equation (either version) and we got $q(x) = -(x - 2)^2$.

Method 2: The **general form** for a quadratic equation is

$$y = ax^2 + bx + c$$

The graph is a parabola whose vertex has x-coordinate $-\dfrac{b}{2a}$. The parabola opens upwards if $a > 0$, and downwards if $a < 0$.

$q(x) = -(x - 2)^2 = -(x^2 - 4x + 4) = -x^2 + 4x - 4$. So

$$-\frac{b}{2a} = -\frac{4}{2(-1)} = 2.$$

Thus the maximum occurs at $x = 2$ (it's a maximum because the parabola opens downwards).

Method 3: For those who know calculus we can use a derivative. The derivative of $q(x) = -(x - 2)^2$ is $q'(x) = -2(x - 2)$. This is zero when $x = 2$.

138

The derivative is positive for $x < 2$ and negative for $x > 2$ which means that the function is increasing for $x < 2$ and decreasing for $x > 2$. Thus, there is a maximum (both relative and absolute) at $x = 2$.

Note: Any of these last 3 methods can be used from the original equation (without picking numbers). For example, using the first method we have the following:

* $q(x) = a(x - h)^2$ is in standard form and thus has a graph that is a parabola with $(h, 0)$ for its vertex. Since $a < 0$ the parabola opens downwards. Thus the maximum occurs when $x = h$, choice (D).

112. Give one possible solution to the equation $\dfrac{1}{x^2+x} - \dfrac{x-6}{x+1} = \dfrac{x+5}{x^2+x}$.

* **Algebraic solution:** $x^2 + x = x(x + 1)$ is the lcd of the fractions that appear in the equation. So let's begin by multiplying each term by $x(x + 1)$:

$$x(x + 1) \cdot \frac{1}{x^2 + x} - x(x + 1) \cdot \frac{x - 6}{x + 1} = x(x + 1) \cdot \frac{x + 5}{x^2 + x}$$

$$1 - x(x - 6) = x + 5$$

$$1 - x^2 + 6x = x + 5$$

$$0 = x^2 - 5x + 4$$

$$0 = (x - 1)(x - 4)$$

So the two possible solutions are **1** or **4**.

Notes: (1) The lcd (least common denominator) of a set of fractions is the lcm (least common multiple) of the denominators.

In this problem the denominators are $x^2 + x = x(x + 1)$ and $x + 1$. So the lcd is $x^2 + x = x(x + 1)$.

(2) Multiplying each side of a rational equation by the lcd of the fractions that appear in the equation gives an equation without any fractions.

(3) Using the distributive property, we see that multiplying each side of an equation by an expression is the same as multiplying each term by that expression.

(4)
$$x(x+1) \cdot \frac{1}{x^2+x} = x(x+1) \cdot \frac{1}{x(x+1)} = 1$$

$$-x(x+1) \cdot \frac{x-6}{x+1} = -x(x-6) = -x^2 + 6x$$

$$x(x+1) \cdot \frac{x+5}{x^2+x} = x(x+1) \cdot \frac{x+5}{x(x+1)} = x + 5$$

(5) Remember to check that neither solution is extraneous at the end. To do these we need only check that 1 and 4 do not make any denominator zero in the original equation.

(6) If a graphing calculator were allowed for this question, an alternative would be to put each side of the equation into your graphing calculator and then to use the intersect feature (see the graphical solution to problem 73 to see how to do this).

113. If $x^2 - 8x = 209$, and $x < 0$, what is the value of $|x + 3|$?

* Algebraic solution: Let's attempt to factor the equation. We begin by subtracting 209 from each side to get $x^2 - 8x - 209 = 0$. We now factor the left hand side to get $(x - 19)(x + 11) = 0$.

So $x = 19$ or $x = -11$. Since we are given $x < 0$, we use $x = -11$.

Finally, we have $|x + 3| = |-11 + 3| = |-8| = \mathbf{8}$.

Notes: (1) There are several ways to solve a quadratic equation. A few are by (i) factoring, (ii) completing the square, (iii) using the quadratic formula, (iv) guessing and checking, (v) creating a table of values in your calculator, (vi) using the graphing features of your calculator.

(2) Whenever you solve a quadratic equation by factoring or by using the quadratic formula, you need to bring everything over to one side of the equation first, leaving 0 on the other side.

(3) It can seem very difficult at first to find the factors of 209, but the following trick can help you find the factors a little easier. Since we have $15^2 = 225 > 209$, it follows that if 209 can be factored, then it has a factor less than 15. Furthermore, since every positive integer can be factored as a product of primes, it follows that we need only check prime numbers less than 15. So we can simply check 209 for divisibility by 2, 3, 5, 7, 11, and 13.

We can use standard divisibility tricks to eliminate 2, 3, and 5 right away. You may want to try 11 next since it is pretty easy to divide by 11. In this case we have $209 \div 11 = 19$. So $209 = 11 \cdot 19$.

If we happen to be allowed to use a calculator for this problem, then we could divide 209 by these numbers very quickly.

(4) The **zero property** of the real numbers says that when you have a product equal to zero, one of the factors must be zero.

In this problem, since $(x - 19)(x + 11) = 0$, we must have $x - 19 = 0$ or $x + 11 = 0$.

(5) Some students may actually find it easier to solve the given quadratic equation by **completing the square**. In this case we *do not* change the form of the equation:

$$x^2 - 8x = 209$$

We take half of -8, which is -4, and square this number to get 16. We add 16 to each side of the equation to get $x^2 - 8x + 16 = 209 + 16$. This is equivalent to $(x - 4)^2 = 225$. We now apply the **square root property** to get $x - 4 = \pm 15$. So $x = 4 \pm 15$. This yields the two solutions $4 + 15 = 19$, and $4 - 15 = -11$.

(6) We can also solve the given quadratic equation using the **quadratic formula**. For this procedure we need to first subtract 209 from each side to get $x^2 - 8x - 209 = 0$.

$$x = \frac{-b \pm \sqrt{b^2 - 4ac}}{2a} = \frac{8 \pm \sqrt{64 + 836}}{2} = \frac{8 \pm \sqrt{900}}{2} = \frac{8 \pm 30}{2} = 4 \pm 15.$$

As in the previous solution we get $x = 19$ or $x = -11$.

Solution by guessing and checking: If we are allowed to use our calculator, there are several other ways to solve the given equation for x. One way is to simply **guess and check** negative values for x. For example, if we substitute -3 in for x on the left hand side of the equation we get $(-3)^2 - 8(-3) = 33$, which is too small. So let's try $x = -8$ next: $(-8)^2 - 8(-8) = 128$. This is still too small, but we're heading in the right direction. We try $x = -11$ to get $(-11)^2 - 8(-11) = 209$.

It works. So $x = -11$ and we have $|x + 3| = |-11 + 3| = |-8| = \mathbf{8}$.

Solution by creating a table of values: Another way to use our calculator to solve this problem is to **create a table of values**. We press the Y= button, and enter the following.

$$Y_1 = X^2 - 8X - 209$$

Now press TABLE (which is 2ND GRAPH).

Since we want a negative value for x, we start scrolling through negative integers until we see 0 in the Y_1 column. This happens when $x = -11$.

Finally, we have $|x + 3| = |-11 + 3| = |-8| = \textbf{8}$.

Solution by graphing: As in the previous solution press the Y= button, and enter the following.

$$Y_1 = X \char`\^ 2 - 8X - 209$$

This time press ZOOM 6 to graph the parabola in a standard window. Uh oh – there's nothing there! Don't worry – we probably just need to zoom out. Press the WINDOW button, and change Xmin to -100, Xmax to 100, Ymin to -100, and Ymax to 100. Then press 2nd TRACE (which is CALC) 2 (or select ZERO).

Now move the cursor just to the left of the negative x-intercept and press ENTER. Now move the cursor just to the right of the negative x-intercept and press ENTER again. Press ENTER once more, and you will see that the x-coordinate of the negative x-intercept is -11.

Finally we have $|x + 3| = |-11 + 3| = |-8| = \textbf{8}$.

Remark: The choices made for Xmax, Ymin and Ymax were just to try to ensure that the negative x-intercept would appear in the viewing window. Many other windows would work just as well.

114. Let $x \therefore y$ be defined as the sum of all integers between x and y. For example, $1 \therefore 4 = 2 + 3 = 5$. What is the value of $(60 \therefore 900) - (63 \therefore 898)$?

* We write out each sum formally, line them up so that the numbers match up, and subtract term by term.

$$61 + 62 + 63 + 64 + \ldots + 897 + 898 + 899$$
$$64 + \ldots + 897$$
$$\overline{61 + 62 + 63 + 0 + \ldots + 0 + 898 + 899}$$

So the answer is $61 + 62 + 63 + 898 + 899 = \textbf{1983}$.

LEVEL 5: PROBLEM SOLVING AND DATA

115. * A survey was conducted among a randomly chosen sample of 250 single men and 250 single women about whether they owned any dogs or cats. The table below displays a summary of the survey results.

	Dogs Only	Cats Only	Both	Neither	Total
Men	92	27	5	126	250
Women	75	43	34	98	250
Total	167	70	39	224	500

According to the table, which of the following statements is most likely to be false?

(A) The probability that a woman is a cat owner is greater than the probability that a cat owner is a woman

(B) The probability that a dog owner is male is greater than the probability that a randomly chosen person is a cat owner.

(C) The probability that a woman does not own a dog or cat is greater than the probability that a man owns at least one dog and one cat.

(D) The probability that a cat owner is a woman is greater than the probability that a man owns a dog.

* We are being asked to use the table to compute **conditional probabilities**. Let's name the **events** we will be referring to in the obvious way. For example, M will stand for "the person is a Man," and D will stand for "the person owns Dogs Only." As an example, the probability that a person owns cats only will be written $P(C)$, and the probability that a woman owns cats only will be written $P(C|W)$. The expression $P(C|W)$ is a conditional probability and should be read "the probability the person owns cats only *given* that the person is a woman," or more succinctly as "the probability a woman owns cats only."

143

Let's start with choice (C) and first compute the probability that a woman does not own a dog or cat. Note that we are *given* that the person is a woman. So we restrict our attention to the second row (the row labeled "Women"), and we see that this probability is $P(N|W) = \frac{98}{250} = .392$.

We next compute the probability that a man owns at least one dog and one cat as $P(B|M) = \frac{5}{250} = .02$.

Since $.392 > .02$, we can eliminate choice (C).

Let's try choice (B) next and first compute the probability that a dog owner is male. This is $P(M|D \cup B) = \frac{92+5}{167+39} = \frac{97}{206} \approx .47$.

We next compute the probability that a person is a cat owner. This is $P(C \cup B) = \frac{70+39}{500} = \frac{109}{500} = .218$.

Since $.47 > .218$, we can eliminate choice (B).

Let's try choice (A) and first compute the probability that a woman is a cat owner. This is $P(C \cup B|W) = \frac{43+34}{250} = \frac{77}{250} = .308$.

We next compute the probability that a cat owner is a woman. This is $P(W|C \cup B) = \frac{43+34}{70+39} = \frac{77}{109} \approx .706$.

Since $.308 < .706$, the answer is choice (A).

Notes: (1) For completeness, let's do the computations for choice (D).

The probability that a cat owner is a woman is $P(W|C \cup B) \approx .706$ and the probability that a man owns a dog is $P(D \cup B|M) = \frac{92+5}{250} = .388$.

(2) $X \cup Y$, read "X union Y" is the event consisting of all outcomes in X or Y. For example, $D \cup B$ is the event consisting of people who own dogs only or both dogs and cats. In other words, $D \cup B$ is the event consisting of people who own dogs.

(3) B is the event consisting of people who own at least 1 dog and 1 cat.

(4) $X \cap Y$, read "X intersect Y" is the event consisting of all outcomes common to both X and Y. For example, $D \cap M$ is the event consisting of people who are men and own dogs, or equivalently, males that have dogs only.

144

(5) $P(X|Y)$ is the probability of X given Y, and can be computed with the formula $P(X|Y) = \frac{P(X \cap Y)}{P(Y)}$.

For example, $P(N|W) = \frac{P(N \cap W)}{P(W)}$.

$P(N \cap W)$ can be found in the table by looking at the entry in the column for Neither and the row for Women. So $P(N \cap W) = \frac{98}{500}$.

We also have $P(W) = \frac{250}{500}$.

It follows that $P(N|W) = \frac{P(N \cap W)}{P(W)} = \frac{98}{500} \div \frac{250}{500} = \frac{98}{500} \cdot \frac{500}{250} = \frac{98}{250} = .392.$

In practice, we can "forget" the 500's and just put 98 over 250.

> 116. Suppose that the average (arithmetic mean) of a, b, and c is h, the average of b, c, and d is j, and the average of d and e is k. What is the average of a and e?
>
> (A) $h - j + k$
>
> (B) $\frac{3h + 3j - 2k}{2}$
>
> (C) $\frac{3h - 3j + 2k}{2}$
>
> (D) $\frac{3h - 3j + 2k}{5}$

* Solution by changing averages to sums and trying a simple operation: We have that $a + b + c = 3h$, $b + c + d = 3j$, and $d + e = 2k$. If we subtract the second equation from the first, and then add the third equation we get $a + e = 3h - 3j + 2k$. So the average of a and e is $\frac{a + e}{2} = \frac{3h - 3j + 2k}{2}$, choice (C).

Solution by picking numbers: Let's choose values for a, b, c, d, and e, say $a = 1$, $b = 2$, $c = 3$, $d = 4$, and $e = 6$. Then $h = 2$, $j = 3$, $k = 5$ and the average of a and e is **3.5**. The answer choices become

(A) 4
(B) 2.5
(C) 3.5
(D) 1.4

Since (A), (B) and (D) came out incorrect, the answer is choice (C).

$$\frac{1}{x^3}, \frac{1}{x^2}, \frac{1}{x}, x^2, x^3$$

117. If $-1 < x < 0$, what is the median of the five numbers in the list above?

(A) $\frac{1}{x^3}$

(B) $\frac{1}{x^2}$

(C) $\frac{1}{x}$

(D) x^3

* Solution by picking a number: Let's choose $x = -\frac{1}{2}$.

Then we have $\frac{1}{x^3} = (-2)^3 = -8$, $\frac{1}{x^2} = (-2)^2 = 4$, $\frac{1}{x} = -2$, $x^2 = \frac{1}{4}$ and $x^3 = \left(-\frac{1}{2}\right)^3 = -\frac{1}{8}$.

Now let's place them in increasing order.

$$-8, -2, -\frac{1}{8}, \frac{1}{4}, 4$$

The median is $-\frac{1}{8}$ which is x^3, choice (D).

Note: If we are allowed to use a calculator for this problem, we can do all the computations in our calculator and get the following decimals:

$$\frac{1}{x^3} = -8 \quad \frac{1}{x^2} = 4 \quad \frac{1}{x} = -2 \quad x^2 = 0.25 \quad x^3 = -0.125$$

Here they are in increasing order:

$$-8, -2, -0.125, 0.25, 4$$

The median is -0.125 which is x^3, choice (D).

146

Questions 118 - 119 refer to the following information.

A biologist places a colony consisting of 5000 bacteria into a petri dish. After the initial placement of the bacteria at time $t = 0$, the biologist measures and estimates the number of bacteria present every half hour. This data was then fitted by an exponential curve of the form $y = c \cdot 2^{kt}$ where c and k are constants, t is measured in hours, and y is measured in thousands of bacteria. The scatterplot together with the exponential curve are shown below.

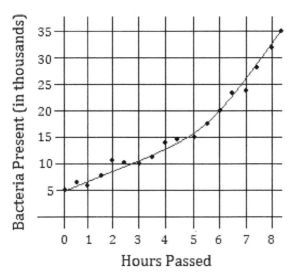

118. According to the scatterplot, the biologist's measurements indicate that the number of bacteria present quadrupled in 6 hours, and the exponential curve passes through the corresponding data point at time $t = 6$. The exponential function also agrees with the initial number of bacteria. Compute ck.

* Since there are 5000 bacteria present at time $t = 0$, we have $c = 5$. So $y = 5 \cdot 2^{kt}$.

We are given that $y = 4 \cdot 5 = 20$ when $t = 6$, so that $20 = 5 \cdot 2^{6k}$. Dividing each side of this equation by 5 yields $4 = 2^{6k}$. So we have $2^2 = 2^{6k}$, and therefore $2 = 6k$. So $k = \frac{2}{6} = \frac{1}{3}$, and $ck = 5 \cdot \frac{1}{3} = \mathbf{5/3}$.

Notes: (1) We can also grid in the decimals **1.66** or **1.67**.

147

(2) Since there are 5000 bacteria present at time $t = 0$, we see that the point $(0,5)$ is a data point. Since the exponential function agrees with the initial number of bacteria, we have that the point $(0,5)$ is also on the exponential curve. So $5 = c \cdot 2^{k \cdot 0} = c$. So $c = 5$.

This computation is not really necessary, because c is always the initial amount in the exponential function $y = c \cdot 2^{kt}$.

(3) After 6 hours, the biologist measured that 20,000 bacteria were present. Since the exponential curve matches the data point at 6 hours, we see that the point $(6,20)$ is both a data point and a point on the exponential curve.

In particular, $20 = 5 \cdot 2^{k \cdot 6} = 5 \cdot 2^{6k}$.

(4) A common mistake is to write $5 \cdot 2^{6k} = 10^{6k}$. The 5 CANNOT be combined in any way with the 2 as this would violate the usual order of operations.

To eliminate the 5, we divide each side of the equation by 5:

$$\frac{20}{5} = \frac{5 \cdot 2^{6k}}{5}$$

$$4 = 2^{6k}$$

(5) The expressions 4 and 2^{6k} both have a common base of 2. Indeed, $4 = 2^2$. So we have $2^2 = 2^{6k}$.

(6) When two expressions have the same base, the exponents must be equal. In this case, since $2^2 = 2^{6k}$, we must have $2 = 6k$.

119. Suppose that the data was fitted with a quadratic function of the form $t^2 + bt + c$ instead of an exponential function. Assume that the quadratic function agrees with the scatterplot at times $t = 0$ and $t = 6$. What is the t-coordinate of the vertex of the graph of the quadratic function?

* Since there are 5000 bacteria present at time $t = 0$, we have $c = 5$. So $y = t^2 + bt + 5$.

According to the scatterplot, $y = 20$ when $t = 6$, so that we have $20 = 6^2 + 6b + 5 = 36 + 6b + 5 = 41 + 6b$. It follows that $6b = 20 - 41 = -21$, and therefore $b = -\frac{21}{6} = -\frac{7}{2}$.

148

The t-coordinate of the vertex of the graph of the quadratic function is

$$\frac{-\left(-\frac{7}{2}\right)}{2\cdot 1} = \frac{7}{2} \div 2 = \frac{7}{2}\cdot\frac{1}{2} = \frac{7}{4} \text{ or } 1.75.$$

Notes: (1) Since the quadratic function agrees with the initial number of bacteria, we have that the point $(0,5)$ is on the quadratic curve. So $5 = 0^2 + b(0) + c = c$. Therefore $c = 5$.

This computation is not really necessary, because c is always the y-coordinate of the y-intercept of the graph of the quadratic equation. $y = at^2 + bt + c$.

(3) The general form for a quadratic function is

$$y = ax^2 + bx + c.$$

The graph of this function is a parabola whose vertex has x-coordinate

$$-\frac{b}{2a}$$

The parabola opens upwards if $a > 0$ and downwards if $a < 0$.

It follows that the graph of $y = t^2 - \frac{7}{2}t + 5$ has a vertex with t-coordinate $-\frac{\left(-\frac{7}{2}\right)}{2(1)} = \frac{7}{4}.$

(4) We can also find the vertex by putting the quadratic function into standard form by completing the square. See problem 90 for more details.

120. * John, a United States resident, is on vacation in Spain and is trying to decide if he should use his own credit card from the U.S., or to purchase a prepaid credit card for 500 euros in Spain.

The bank that issues John's U.S. credit card converts all purchase prices at the foreign exchange rate for that day, and an additional fee of 6% of the converted cost is applied before the bank posts the charge.

If John decides to purchase the prepaid card, he can use this card spending dollars at the exchange rate for that day with no fee, but he loses any money left unspent on the card.

Suppose that John does decide to buy the prepaid card. What is the least number of the 500 euros John must spend for the prepaid card to have been the cheaper option? Round your answer to the nearest whole number of euros.

* If we let d be the cost of the 500 euro card in dollars, and we let e be John's total purchases on the prepaid card in euros, we need

$$d < 1.06 \left(\frac{d}{500}\right) e$$

We can divide each side of this inequality by d to get $1 < e \left(\frac{1.06}{500}\right)$, and then multiply each side of this last equation by $\frac{500}{1.06}$ to get $\frac{500}{1.06} < e$, or equivalently $e > 471.698$.

So the least number of the 500 euros John must spend is **472**.

Notes: (1) Since John is paying d dollars for the prepaid 500 euro card, it follows that the exchange rate on this particular day is $\frac{d}{500}$.

(2) Since John's total purchases on the prepaid card was e euros, it follows that John spent $\left(\frac{d}{500}\right) e$ dollars.

(3) If John spent the e euros on his U.S. credit card instead, he would have paid $1.06 \left(\frac{d}{500}\right) e$ dollars because of the extra 6% fee.

(4) So d is the cost of the 500 euro prepaid card, and $1.06 \left(\frac{d}{500}\right) e$ is the cost in dollars of spending e euros using the U.S. credit card.

Since we want the cost of the prepaid card to be cheaper, we have the inequality $d < 1.06 \left(\frac{d}{500}\right) e$.

(5) Since d is a factor on each side of the inequality, we can divide each side by d to eliminate this variable. Be careful here! When performing this type of division, it is important that we know that d cannot be zero.

(6) After dividing out the d's, we are left with $1 < 1.06 \left(\frac{1}{500}\right) e$, which we can rewrite as $1 < \left(\frac{1.06}{500}\right) e$.

(7) We can solve the inequality $1 < \left(\frac{1.06}{500}\right) e$ for e by multiplying by the reciprocal of $\frac{1.06}{500}$. The reciprocal of $\frac{1.06}{500}$ is $\frac{500}{1.06}$.

Supplemental Problems
Questions

Full solutions to these problems are available for free download here:
www.thesatmathprep.com/NewSAT2016.html

LEVEL 1: HEART OF ALGEBRA

1. A caterer is hired to provide food for a private party consisting of 20 businessmen. She will be paid $80 per hour and an additional $40 tip if she serves all the food on time. If the caterer serves all the food on time, which of the following expressions can be used to determine how much the caterer earns, in dollars?

   (A) $40x + (80 + 20)$, where x is the number of businessmen
   (B) $(80 + 20)x + 40$, where x is the number of businessmen
   (C) $40x + 80$, where x is the number of hours
   (D) $80x + 40$, where x is the number of hours

2. If Edna drove s miles in t hours, which of the following represents her average speed, in miles per hour?

   (A) $\frac{s}{t}$

   (B) $\frac{t}{s}$

   (C) $\frac{1}{st}$

   (D) st

3. A supermarket sells protein cookies individually and in packs of 12. During a certain week, the supermarket sold a total of 315 protein cookies, of which 51 were sold individually. Which expression gives the number of packs of cookies sold during that week?

   (A) $\frac{315}{12} + 51$

   (B) $\frac{315}{12} - 51$

   (C) $\frac{315+51}{12}$

   (D) $\frac{315-51}{12}$

151

4.   Which of the following mathematical expressions is equivalent to the verbal expression "A number, c, squared is 52 more than the product of c and 11"?

  (A) $2c = 52 + 11c$
  (B) $2c = 52c + 11c$
  (C) $c^2 = 52 - 11c$
  (D) $c^2 = 52 + 11c$

5.   For what value of x is $\frac{3x}{7} - 11 = 16$?

6.   If $18x + 42y = 66$, what is the value of $3x + 7y$?

LEVEL 1: GEOMETRY AND TRIG

7.   In the standard (x, y) coordinate plane, what is the slope of the line segment joining the points $(3, -5)$ and $(7, 2)$?

  (A) $-\frac{7}{4}$

  (B) $-\frac{3}{4}$

  (C) $\frac{3}{4}$

  (D) $\frac{7}{4}$

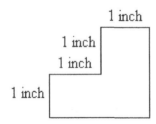

8.   How many figures of the size and shape above are needed to completely cover a rectangle measuring 60 inches by 40 inches?

  (A) 400
  (B) 600
  (C) 800
  (D) 1000

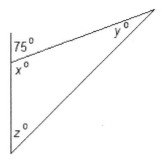

9. In the figure above, one side of a triangle is extended. Which of the following is true?

    (A) $y = 75$
    (B) $z = 75$
    (C) $z - y = 75$
    (D) $y + z = 75$

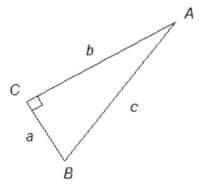

10. The dimensions of the right triangle above are given in meters. What is $\tan B$?

    (A) $\dfrac{c}{b}$
    (B) $\dfrac{a}{b}$
    (C) $\dfrac{a}{c}$
    (D) $\dfrac{b}{a}$

153

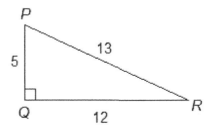

11. In $\triangle PQR$ above, which of the following trigonometric expressions has value $\frac{12}{13}$?

   (A) $\tan P$
   (B) $\cos P$
   (C) $\sin R$
   (D) $\cos R$

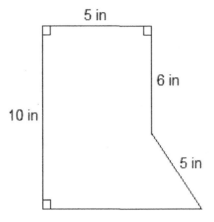

12. What is the perimeter of polygon $PQRST$ shown above, in inches?

LEVEL 1: PASSPORT TO ADVANCED MATH

13. For the function $f(x) = 5x^2 - 7x$, what is the value of $f(-3)$?

   (A) -66
   (B) -24
   (C) 24
   (D) 66

14. If $3x^2 + 9x = 84$, what are the possible values for x ?

    (A) -4 and 7
    (B) -7 and 4
    (C) -7 and -4
    (D) -7 and -12

15. A rectangle has area A, length l, and width w. Which of the following represents w in terms of A and l ?

    (A) $w = \dfrac{A}{2l}$

    (B) $w = \dfrac{A}{l}$

    (C) $w = \dfrac{2A}{l}$

    (D) $w = \dfrac{\sqrt{A}}{l}$

16. For which nonnegative value of b is the expression $\dfrac{1}{2-b^2}$ undefined?

    (A) 0
    (B) $\sqrt{2}$
    (C) 2
    (D) 8

$$f(x) = 7x - 3$$
$$g(x) = x^2 - 2x + 6$$

17. The functions f and g are defined above. What is the value of $f(11) - g(4)$?

x	$p(x)$	$q(x)$	$r(x)$
1	4	5	9
2	-2	6	-9
3	-5	-9	4
4	-3	-10	-7
5	-5	0	-5

18. The table above gives some values of the functions p, q, and r. At which value x does $q(x) = p(x) + r(x)$?

155

LEVEL 1: PROBLEM SOLVING AND DATA

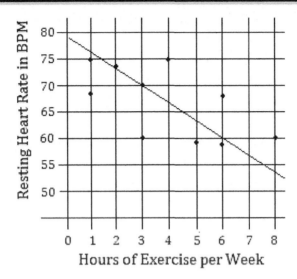

19. Ten 25-year-old men were asked how many hours per week they exercise and their resting heart rate was taken in beats per minute (BPM). The results are shown as points in the scatterplot above, and the line of best fit is drawn. What is the resting heart rate, in BPM, of the man represented by the data point that is farthest from the line of best fit?

    (A) 60
    (B) 66
    (C) 67
    (D) 75

156

20. A survey was conducted among a randomly chosen sample of 100 males and 100 females to gather data on family size. The data are shown in the table below.

	Have siblings	Do not have siblings	Total
Men	75	25	100
Women	63	37	100
Total	138	62	200

Which of the following is closest to the percent of those surveyed who have siblings?

(A) 31
(B) 63
(C) 69
(D) 75

21. For which of the following lists of 5 numbers is the average (arithmetic mean) greater than the median?

(A) 3, 3, 5, 8, 8
(B) 2, 3, 5, 6, 7
(C) 3, 3, 5, 7, 7
(D) 3, 4, 5, 6, 7

22. A 770-gallon tank is filled to capacity with water. At most how many 14 ounce bottles can be filled with water from the tank? (1 gallon = 128 ounces)

23. Running at a constant speed, an antelope traveled 150 miles in 6 hours. At this rate, how many miles did the antelope travel in 5 hours?

24. What is the median of the following 9 test grades?

95, 72, 81, 96, 62, 98, 82, 76, 82

157

LEVEL 2: HEART OF ALGEBRA

25. Which of the following is equal to $\frac{x+48}{12}$?

   (A) $\frac{x+24}{6}$

   (B) $x + 4$

   (C) $4x$

   (D) $\frac{x}{12} + 4$

$$\frac{1}{3}x - \frac{1}{6}y = 7$$

$$\frac{1}{5}y - \frac{1}{5}x = 8$$

26. Which of the following ordered pairs (x, y) satisfies the system of equations above?

   (A) $(-36, -57)$

   (B) $(12, 43)$

   (C) $(\frac{101}{5}, \frac{307}{5})$

   (D) $(82, 122)$

$$T = 25 + 3c$$

27. The equation above is used to model the number of chirps, c, made by a certain species of cricket in one minute, and the temperature, T, in degrees Fahrenheit. According to this model, what is the meaning of the number 3 in the equation.

   (A) If a cricket chirps three more times in one minute, then the temperature, in Fahrenheit, will be one degree higher.

   (B) If a cricket chirps three fewer times in one minute, then the temperature, in Fahrenheit, will be one degree higher.

   (C) If a cricket chirps one more time in one minute, then the temperature, in Fahrenheit, will be three degrees higher.

   (D) If a cricket chirps one fewer time in one minute, then the temperature, in Fahrenheit, will be three degrees higher.

28. Gina subscribes to a cell phone service that charges a monthly fee of $60.00. The first 500 megabytes of data is free, and the cost is $0.15 for each additional megabyte of data used that month. Which of the following functions gives the cost, in dollars, for a month in which Gina uses x megabytes of data, where $x > 500$.

(A) $60 + 15x$
(B) $0.15x - 15$
(C) $0.15x - 440$
(D) $60 + 0.15x$

$$50t + 3c = 300$$

29. Robert is playing blackjack at a casino. The equation above can be used to model the number of chips, c, that Robert still has in his possession t hours after he begins playing. What does it mean that $t = 0$, $c = 100$ is a solution to this equation?

(A) Robert is losing 10 chips per hour.
(B) It would take 100 hours for Robert to have 300 chips.
(C) Robert can play for 100 hours before losing all his chips.
(D) Robert begins playing with 100 chips.

30. At a pet store, each frog is priced at $1 and each salamander is priced at $8. Jeff purchased 14 amphibians at the store for a total price of $42. How many frogs did Jeff purchase?

LEVEL 2: GEOMETRY AND TRIG

31. If each base of a trapezoid is reduced by 50% and the height of the trapezoid is quadrupled, how would the area of the trapezoid change?

(A) The area would be multiplied by 4.
(B) The area would be multiplied by 2.
(C) The area would not change.
(D) The area would be cut in half.

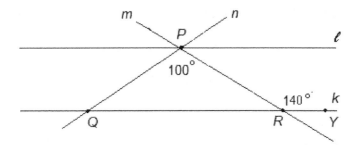

32. In the figure above, line ℓ is parallel to line k. Transversals m
     and n intersect at point P on ℓ and intersect k at points R and Q,
     respectively. Point Y is on k, the measure of $\angle PRY$ is 140°, and
     the measure of $\angle QPR$ is 100°. How many of the angles formed
     by rays ℓ, k, m, and n have measure 40° ?

     (A) 4
     (B) 6
     (C) 8
     (D) 10

33. In the xy-plane, the point $(0, 2)$ is the center of a circle that has
     radius 2. Which of the following is NOT a point on the circle?

     (A) $(0, 4)$
     (B) $(-2, 4)$
     (C) $(-2, 2)$
     (D) $(0, 0)$

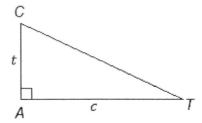

34. Given $\triangle CAT$ above, which of the following is equal to $\dfrac{t}{c}$?

     (A) $\cos C$
     (B) $\cos T$
     (C) $\tan C$
     (D) $\tan T$

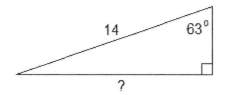

35. The figure above shows a 14-foot ramp that forms an angle of 63° with the vertical wall it is leaning against. Which of the following is an expression for the horizontal length, in feet, of the ramp?

    (A) 14 cos 63°
    (B) 14 sin 63°
    (C) 14 tan 63°
    (D) 14 cot 63°

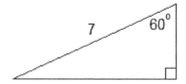

36. The figure above shows a right triangle whose hypotenuse is 7 feet long. How many feet long is the longer leg of this triangle?

    (A) 3.5
    (B) 14
    (C) $\frac{7\sqrt{3}}{2}$
    (D) $\frac{7\sqrt{3}}{6}$

LEVEL 2: PASSPORT TO ADVANCED MATH

37. The expression $(3b - 2)(b + 5)$ is equivalent to:

    (A) $3b^2 - 7$
    (B) $3b^2 - 10$
    (C) $3b^2 - 2b - 7$
    (D) $3b^2 + 13b - 10$

38. The value of x that will make $\frac{x}{3} - 2 = -\frac{11}{4}$ a true statement lies between which of the following numbers?

    (A) -3 and -2
    (B) -2 and -1
    (C) -1 and 0
    (D) 0 and 1

39. If $g(x - 3) = 5x + 1$ for all values of x, what is the value of $g(-2)$?

40. What is the value of $c - 2$ if $(3c - 7) - (3 - 2c) = 5$?

41. The operation $\blacksquare$ is defined as $a \blacksquare b = \frac{2b^2 - 8a^2}{b + 2a}$ where a and b are real numbers and $b \neq -2a$. What is the value of $(-2) \blacksquare (-1)$?

42. Let a function of 2 variables be defined by $g(x, y) = xy + 3xy^2 - (x - y^2)$, what is the value of $g(2, -1)$?

LEVEL 2: PROBLEM SOLVING AND DATA

43. Exactly 52% of the marbles in a jar are red. Which of the following could be the total number of marbles in the jar?

    (A) 20
    (B) 21
    (C) 25
    (D) 28

162

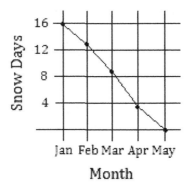

Month

44. The line graph above shows the average number of days that it snows at least 0.1 inch in Buffalo, NY from January to May. According to the graph, approximately what was the greatest decrease in the number of snow days from one month to the next month?

(A) 2
(B) 3
(C) 4
(D) 6

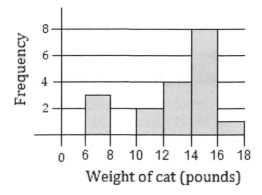

Weight of cat (pounds)

45. The histogram above shows the distribution of the weights, in pounds, of 18 cats in a shelter. Which of the following could be the median weight of the 18 cats represented in the histogram?

(A) 10 pounds
(B) 11 pounds
(C) 13.5 pounds
(D) 16 pounds

46. Jeff has taken 6 of 10 equally weighted math tests this semester, and he has an average score of exactly 82.0 points. How many points does he need to earn on the 7th test to bring his average score up to exactly 83 points?

47. A group of 286 parents is to be divided into committees with 3 or more parents on each committee. If each committee must have the same number of parents and every parent must be on a committee what is the maximum number of committees possible?

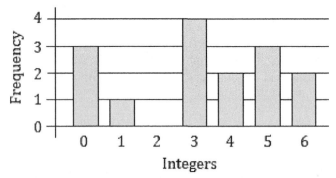

48. * The graph above shows the frequency distribution of a list of randomly generated integers between 0 and 6. What is the mean of the list of numbers?

LEVEL 3: HEART OF ALGEBRA

49. Michael needs a printing job completed. Photoperfect Print Shop charges a fixed fee of $3 for the print job and 5 cents per page. Bargain Printing charges a fixed fee of $2 for the print job and 7 cents per page. If p represents the number of pages being printed, what are all values of p for which Photoperfect Print Shop's total charge is less than Bargain Printing's total charge.

(A) $p < 20$
(B) $20 \le p \le 35$
(C) $35 \le p \le 50$
(D) $p > 50$

50. Which of the following is equivalent to $(\frac{ab}{c})(cb - a)$?

  (A) $ab^2 - \frac{b}{c}$

  (B) $ab^2 - \frac{a^2b}{c}$

  (C) $\frac{ab}{c} - \frac{a^2b}{c}$

  (D) $\frac{ab}{c} - a^2bc$

51. A block is sliding down a ramp that drops 3 centimeters in elevation for every 5 centimeters along the length of the ramp. The top of the ramp, where the back edge of the block is initially placed, is at 60 centimeters elevation, and the block is sliding at 10 centimeters per second down the ramp. What is the elevation of the ramp, in centimeters, at the point where the back of the block passes t seconds after being released?

  (A) $60 - \frac{3}{5}t$

  (B) $60 - 3t$

  (C) $60 - 6t$

  (D) $60 - 9t$

52. It costs $(s + t)$ dollars for a box of brand A cat food, and $(q - r)$ dollars for a box of brand B cat food. The difference between the cost of 15 boxes of brand A cat food and 7 boxes of brand B cat food is k dollars. Which of the following equations represents a relationship between s, t, q, r, and k ?

  (A) $105(s + t)(q - r) = k$
  (B) $|7(q - r) + 15(s - t)| = k$
  (C) $|15(s + t) + 7(q - r)| = k$
  (D) $|15(s + t) - 7(q - r)| = k$

53. Tickets for a concert cost $4.00 for children and $6.00 for adults. 850 concert tickets were sold for a total cost of $3820. How many children's tickets were sold?

54. * If $(\sqrt{x})^y = 5$, what is the value of $\frac{1}{x^{2y}}$?

165

LEVEL 3: GEOMETRY AND TRIG

55. Which of the following is an equation of the line in the xy-plane that passes through the point $(0, -7)$ and is perpendicular to the line $y = -6x + 2$?

(A) $y = -6x + 7$

(B) $y = -6x + 14$

(C) $y = -\frac{1}{6}x + 6$

(D) $y = \frac{1}{6}x - 7$

56. Line k contains the point $(4,0)$ and has slope 5. Which of the following points is on line k?

(A) $(1, 5)$

(B) $(3, 5)$

(C) $(5, 5)$

(D) $(7, 5)$

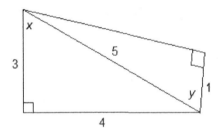

57. The 2 triangles in the figure above share a common side. What is $\cos(x + y)$?

(Note: $\cos(x + y) = \cos x \cos y - \sin x \sin y$ for all x and y.)

(A) $\frac{4}{5}$

(B) $\frac{3 + 4\sqrt{24}}{5}$

(C) $\frac{4\sqrt{24} - 3}{25}$

(D) $\frac{3 - 4\sqrt{24}}{25}$

58. The sum of the areas of two squares is 85. If the sides of both squares have integer lengths, what is the least possible value for the length of a side of the smaller square?

166

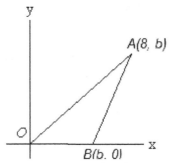

Note: Figure not drawn to scale.

59. In the xy-plane above, the area of triangle OAB is 32. What is the value of b?

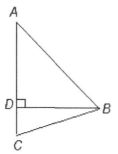

Note: Figure not drawn to scale.

60. Triangle ABC has the same area as a rectangle with sides of lengths 5 and 7. If the length of $\overline{AC}$ is 10, what is the length of $\overline{BD}$?

LEVEL 3: PASSPORT TO ADVANCED MATH

$$7(a + b) = 2(b - a)$$

61. If (a, b) is a solution to the equation above and $a \neq 0$, what is the ratio $\frac{b}{a}$?

(A) $-\frac{9}{5}$

(B) $-\frac{8}{5}$

(C) 8

(D) 11

$$h(x) = -2(x^2 - 5x + 3) + 7(c - x)$$

62. In the polynomial $h(x)$ defined above, c is a constant. If $h(x)$ is divisible by x, what is the value of c ?

  (A) $-\frac{6}{7}$

  (B) 0

  (C) $\frac{6}{7}$

  (D) 6

63. For all x, $(x^2 - 3x + 1)(x + 2) = ?$

  (A) $x^3 - x^2 - 5x + 2$
  (B) $x^3 - x^2 - 5x - 2$
  (C) $x^3 - x^2 + 5x + 2$
  (D) $x^3 + x^2 - 5x + 2$

64. For all numbers a and b, let $a \triangledown b = a^2 - 3ab^2$. What is the value of $|5 \triangledown (2 \triangledown 1)|$?

65. If $k \neq 0$, what is the value of $\frac{9(2k)^3}{(3k)^3}$?

66. For any real numbers r and s such that $r \neq s$, let $r \cdots s$ be defined by $r \cdots s = \frac{r-s}{r+s}$. If $r - s = 63$ and $r \cdots s = 9$, what is the value of r ?

LEVEL 3: PROBLEM SOLVING AND DATA

67. Which scatterplot shows a nonlinear positive association? (Note: A positive association between two variables is one in which higher values of one variable correspond to higher values of the other variable.)

(A)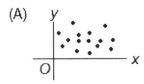

(B)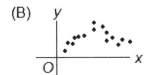

(C)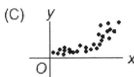

(D)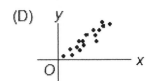

68. The average (arithmetic mean) age of the people in a certain group was 35 years before one of the members left the group and was replaced by someone who is 12 years older than the person who left. If the average age of the group is now 37 years, how many people are in the group?

69. A mixture is made by combining a red liquid and a blue liquid so that the ratio of the red liquid to the blue liquid is 17 to 3 by weight. How many liters of the blue liquid are needed to make a 420-liter mixture?

70. A bus driver drove at an average speed of 45 miles per hour for 3 hours while the bus consumed fuel at a rate of 15 miles per gallon. How many gallons of fuel did the bus use for the entire 3-hour trip?

TEST GRADES OF STUDENTS IN MATH CLASS

Test Grade	75	82	87	93	100
Number of students with that grade	5	7	10	3	1

71. The test grades of the 26 students in a math class are shown in the chart above. What is the median test grade for the class?

72. A certain exam lasts a total of 4 hours. Each part of the exam requires the same amount of time and 10 minute breaks are included between consecutive parts. If there is a total of 4 breaks during the 4 hours, what is the required time, in minutes, for each part of the test?

LEVEL 4: HEART OF ALGEBRA

$$\frac{5}{\sqrt{x-7}} = 6$$

73. For $x > 7$, which of the following equations is equivalent to the equation above?

(A) $25 = 36(x - 7)$
(B) $25 = 6(x - 7)$
(C) $25 = 6(x - \sqrt{7})$
(D) $5 = 36(x - 7)$

$$x = 36z$$
$$y = 36z^2 + 5$$

74. If $z > 0$ in the equations above, what is y in terms of x?

(A) $y = \dfrac{1}{36}x^2 + 4$

(B) $y = \dfrac{1}{36}x^2 + 5$

(C) $y = \dfrac{1}{36}x^2 + 36$

(D) $y = \dfrac{1}{6}x^2 + 4$

75. A small hotel has 15 rooms which are all occupied. If each room is occupied by either one or two guests and there are 27 guests in total, how many rooms are occupied by two guests?

$$x + 2y = 3$$
$$2x - y = 8.5$$

76. If (x, y) is a solution to the above system of equations, what is the value of $x - y$?

77. If $xy = 22, yz = 10, xz = 55$, and $x > 0$, then $xyz =$

78. Last month Joe the painter painted many rooms. He used 3 coats of paint on one third of the rooms he painted. On two fifths of the remaining rooms he used 2 coats of paint, and he only used 1 coat of paint on the remaining 24 rooms. What was the total number of coats of paint Joe painted last month?

LEVEL 4: GEOMETRY AND TRIG

79. A cylinder has volume V, height h, and base diameter d. Which of the following represents d in terms of V and h?

(A) $d = \sqrt{V\pi h}$

(B) $d = \sqrt{\dfrac{V}{\pi h}}$

(C) $d = \sqrt{\dfrac{2V}{\pi h}}$

(D) $d = \sqrt{\dfrac{4V}{\pi h}}$

80. When each side of a given square is lengthened by 3 inches, the area is increased by 45 square inches. What is the length, in inches, of a side of the original square?

    (A) 3
    (B) 4
    (C) 5
    (D) 6

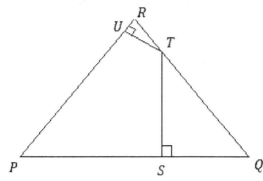

Note: Figure not drawn to scale.

81. Triangle PQR above is equilateral with $PQ = 44$. The ratio of ST to TU is $8:3$. What is the length of $\overline{SQ}$?

    (A) 6
    (B) 16
    (C) $16\sqrt{3}$
    (D) 32

82. A 7-foot ladder is leaning against a wall such that the angle relative to the level ground is 70°. Which of the following expressions involving cosine gives the distance, in feet, from the base of the ladder to the wall?

    (A) $\dfrac{7}{\cos 70°}$

    (B) $\dfrac{\cos 70°}{7}$

    (C) $\dfrac{1}{7\cos 70°}$

    (D) $7\cos 70°$

171

83. The length of each side of an equilateral triangle will be doubled to create a second triangle. The area of the second triangle will be how many times the area of the original triangle?

84. In triangle DEF, $DE = DF = 10$ and $EF = 16$. What is the area of the triangle?

LEVEL 4: PASSPORT TO ADVANCED MATH

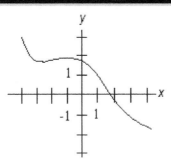

85. What is the maximum value of the function graphed on the xy-plane above, for $-4 \leq x \leq 4$?

    (A) -4
    (B) 3
    (C) 4
    (D) ∞

86. Let $\|x\|$ be defined as the sum of the integers from 1 to x, inclusive. Which of the following equals $\|21\| - \|20\|$?

    (A) $\|1\|$
    (B) $\|5\|$
    (C) $\|6\|$
    (D) $\|21\|$

87. In the standard (x, y) coordinate plane, what are the coordinates of the center of the circle whose equation is

$$x^2 - 8x + y^2 + 10y + 15 = 0 ?$$

    (A) $(4,5)$
    (B) $(4, -5)$
    (C) $(-4,5)$
    (D) $(-5, -4)$

172

88. If $\frac{x^a x^b}{(x^c)^d} = x^2$ for all $x \neq 0$, which of the following must be true?

   (A) $a + b - cd = 2$

   (B) $\frac{a+b}{cd} = 2$

   (C) $ab - cd = 2$

   (D) $ab - c^d = 2$

89. In the equation $x^2 - bx + c = 0$, b and c are integers. The solutions of this equation are 2 and 3. What is $c - b$?

$$3x^2 + 19x = 14$$

90. If a and b are distinct solutions of the equation above, what is the value of $-3ab$?

LEVEL 4: PROBLEM SOLVING AND DATA

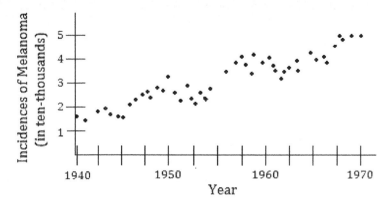

91. The scatterplot above shows the numbers of people diagnosed with melanoma, in ten-thousands, from 1940 to 1970. Based on the data shown in the figure, which of the following values is closest to the range of the number of incidences of melanoma between 1945 and 1950?

   (A) 5,000
   (B) 10,000
   (C) 17,000
   (D) 36,000

173

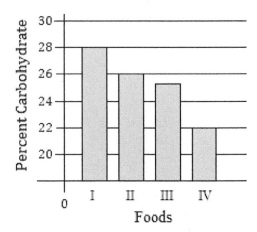

Percent Carbohydrate in Four Foods

92. * The graph above shows the amount of carbohydrate supplied by four different foods, I, II, III, and IV, as a percentage of their total weights. The cost of 20 ounces of foods I, II, III, and IV, are $4.00, $3.50, $3.00, and $2.75, respectively. Which of the four foods supplies the most carbohydrate per dollar?

(A) I
(B) II
(C) III
(D) IV

93. In Dr. Steve's math class, 12 students play the piano and 17 students play the guitar. If a total of 19 students play only one of these two instruments, how many students play both instruments?

174

94. * 743 children from the United States, aged 6 through 11, were tested to see if they were overweight. The data are shown in the table below.

	Overweight	Not overweight	Total
Ages 6-8	31	286	317
Ages 9-11	163	263	426
Total	194	549	743

Based on the data, how many times more likely is it for a 6, 7, or 8-year-old to NOT be overweight than it is for a 9, 10, or 11-year-old to NOT be overweight? (Round the answer to the nearest tenth.)

95. * Jessica has two cats named Mittens and Fluffy. Last year Mittens weighed 12 pounds, and Fluffy weighed 19 pounds. Fluffy was placed on a diet, and his weight decreased by 20%. Mittens weight has increased by 20%. By what percentage did Mitten's and Fluffy's combined weight decrease, to the nearest tenth of a percent?

SURVEY RESULTS

96. The circle graph above shows the distribution of responses to a survey in which a group of people were asked how often they donate to charity. What fraction of those surveyed reported that they donate at least yearly?

175

LEVEL 5: HEART OF ALGEBRA

97. If $x^2 + y^2 = k^2$, and $xy = 8 - 4k$, what is $(x + y)^2$ in terms of k?

    (A) $k - 4$
    (B) $(k - 4)^2$
    (C) $k^2 - 4k + 8$
    (D) $(k - 2)^2 + 4$

$$y \leq 2x + 2$$
$$y \geq -3x - 3$$

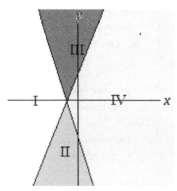

98. A system of inequalities and a graph are shown above. Which section or sections of the graph could represent all of the solutions to the system?

    (A) Section I
    (B) Section IV
    (C) Sections II and III
    (D) Sections I, II, and IV

99. For how many integers n is $(7n - 26)(5n + 11)$ a negative number?

    (A) None
    (B) Two
    (C) Four
    (D) Six

100. If a and b are positive integers, which of the following is equivalent to $(5a)^{3b} - (5a)^{2b}$?

(A) $5^b(a^3 - a^2)$
(B) $(5a)^{2b}[(5a)^{3b} - 1]$
(C) $(5a)^{2b}(25a - 1)$
(D) $(5a)^{2b}[(5a)^b - 1]$

101. If $|-3a + 15| = 6$ and $|-2b + 12| = 4$, what is the greatest possible value of ab?

102. * A cheetah ran 12 miles at an average rate of 50 miles per hour and then ran the next 12 miles at an average rate of 43 miles per hour. What was the average speed, in miles per hour, of the cheetah for the 24 miles?

LEVEL 5: GEOMETRY AND TRIG

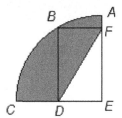

Note: Figure not drawn to scale.

103. In the figure above, arc ABC is one quarter of a circle with center E and radius $8\sqrt{2}$. If the length plus the width of rectangle $BDEF$ is 16, then the area of the shaded region is

(A) $32\pi - 32$
(B) $32\pi - 16$
(C) $32\pi - 8$
(D) $32\pi + 16$

104. A ladder rests against the side of a wall and reaches a point that is h meters above the ground. The angle formed by the ladder and the ground is $\theta°$. A point on the ladder is k meters from the wall. What is the vertical distance, in meters, from this point on the ladder to the ground?

   (A) $(h - k) \tan \theta°$
   (B) $(h - k) \cos \theta°$
   (C) $h - k \sin \theta°$
   (D) $h - k \tan \theta°$

105. * In the xy plane, line k has equation $y = \frac{2}{9}x + 5$, and line n has equation $y = \frac{1}{4}x + b$. If the lines intersect at the point with coordinates $(a, \frac{2}{3})$, what is the value of b ?

106. If the length of a rectangle is increased by 40%, and the width of the same rectangle is decreased by 40%, then the area of the rectangle is decreased by x%. What is the value of x?

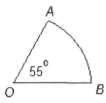

107. * In the figure above, AB is the arc of a circle with center O. If the length of arc AB is 7π, what is the area of region OAB to the nearest integer?

108. A sphere with volume 36π cubic inches is inscribed in a cube so that the sphere touches the cube at 6 points. What is the surface area, in square inches, of the cube?

LEVEL 5: PASSPORT TO ADVANCED MATH

109. * Jonathon wants to place a rectangular fence around the border to his backyard. The width of the fence will be 350 inches more than 5 times the length of the fence. What will be the perimeter of Jonathon's fence if the area of the fence is 64,680 square inches?

(A) 854 inches
(B) 1274 inches
(C) 1708 inches
(D) 2548 inches

110. If a, h, and k are nonzero constants, and the parabola with equation $y = a(x - h)^2 + k$, in the xy-plane, passes through the points $(h, 5)$ and $(0,2)$, which of the following must be true?

(A) $h^2 = -\dfrac{3}{a}$

(B) $a^2 = -\dfrac{3}{h}$

(C) $a = -\dfrac{3}{h}$

(D) $ah = -3$

111. If $x - 3$ is a factor of $ax^2 - a^2x + 12$, where a is a positive constant, what is the value of a ?

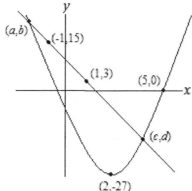

112. The xy-plane above shows the two points of intersection of the graphs of a linear function and a quadratic function. The leftmost point of intersection has coordinates (a, b) and the rightmost point of intersection has coordinates (c, d). If the vertex of the graph of the quadratic function is at $(2, -27)$, what is the value of $b - d$?

179

113. *An arrow is launched upward with an initial speed of 70 m/s (meters per second). The equation $v^2 = v_0^2 - 2gh$ describes the motion of the arrow, where v_0 is the initial speed of the arrow, v is the speed of the arrow as it is moving up in the air, h is the height of the arrow above the ground, t is the time elapsed since the arrow was projected upward, and g is the acceleration due to gravity (approximately 9.8 m/s²). What is the maximum height from the ground the arrow will rise to the nearest meter?

114. Let f be a linear function such that $f(5) = -2$ and $f(11) = 28$. What is the value of $\frac{f(9)-f(7)}{2}$?

LEVEL 5: PROBLEM SOLVING AND DATA

Questions 115 - 116 refer to the following information.

743 children from the United States, aged 6 through 11, were tested to see if they were overweight. The data are shown in the table below.

	Overweight	Not overweight	Total
Ages 6-8	31	286	317
Ages 9-11	163	263	426
Total	194	549	743

115. In 2014 the total population of children between 6 and 11 years old, inclusive, in the United Sates was about 74.3 million. If the test results are used to estimate information about children across the country, which of the following is the best estimate of the total number of children between 9 and 11 years old in the United States who were overweight in 2014?

(A) 3,100,000
(B) 16,300,000
(C) 19,400,000
(D) 42,600,000

116. * According to the table, which of the following statements is most likely to be true about children between 6 and 11 years old, inclusive, in the United Sates?

    (A) The probability that a 6-8 year old is overweight is greater than the probability that an overweight child aged 6-11 is less than 9 years old.

    (B) The probability that a 6-11 year old is overweight is greater than the probability that a 9-11 year old is not overweight.

    (C) The probability that an overweight 6-11 year old is at least 9 years old is greater than the probability that a 6-11 year old is not overweight.

    (D) The probability that a 6-8 year old is overweight is greater than the probability that a 9-11 year old is not overweight.

$$\frac{1}{x^3}, \frac{1}{x^2}, \frac{1}{x}, x, x^2, x^3$$

117. If $-1 < x < 0$, what is the median of the six numbers in the list above?

    (A) $\frac{1}{x}$

    (B) x^2

    (C) $\frac{x^2(x+1)}{2}$

    (D) $\frac{x(x^2+1)}{2}$

118. A group of students takes a test and the average score is 72. One more student takes the test and receives a score of 88 increasing the average score of the group to 76. How many students were in the initial group?

119. Jason ran a race of 1600 meters in two laps of equal distance. His average speeds for the first and second laps were 11 meters per second and 7 meters per second, respectively. What was his average speed for the entire race, in meters per second?

120. A scatterplot includes the points (1,0), (2,0), (3,0), and (0,−6). The data is fitted with a cubic curve whose equation has the form $y = x^3 + bx^2 + cx + d$. If the curve passes through all four of the given points, find the value of $b + c$.

181

ANSWERS TO
SUPPLEMENTAL PROBLEMS

Full explanations are available for free download here:
www.thesatmathprep.com/NewSAT2016.html

LEVEL 1: HEART OF ALGEBRA

1. D
2. A
3. D
4. D
5. 63
6. 11

LEVEL 1: GEOMETRY AND TRIG

7. D
8. C
9. D
10. D
11. D
12. 34

LEVEL 1: PASSPORT TO ADVANCED MATH

13. D
14. B
15. B
16. B
17. 60
18. 4

LEVEL 1: PROBLEM SOLVING AND DATA

19. A
20. C
21. A
22. 7040

23. 125
24. 82

LEVEL 2: HEART OF ALGEBRA

25. D
26. D
27. C
28. B
29. D
30. 10

LEVEL 2: GEOMETRY AND TRIG

31. B
32. C
33. B
34. D
35. B
36. C

LEVEL 2: PASSPORT TO ADVANCED MATH

37. D
38. A
39. 6
40. 1
41. 6
42. 3

LEVEL 2: PROBLEM SOLVING AND DATA

43. C
44. D
45. C
46. 89
47. 26
48. 3.2

LEVEL 3: HEART OF ALGEBRA

49. D
50. B
51. C
52. D
53. 640
54. .001 or .002

LEVEL 3: GEOMETRY AND TRIG

55. D
56. C
57. D
58. 2
59. 8
60. 7

LEVEL 3: PASSPORT TO ADVANCED MATH

61. A
62. C
63. A
64. 35
65. 8/3, 2.66, or 2.67
66. 35

LEVEL 3: PROBLEM SOLVING AND DATA

67. C
68. 6
69. 63
70. 9
71. 87
72. 40

LEVEL 4: HEART OF ALGEBRA

73. A
74. B
75. 12
76. 9/2 or 4.5
77. 110
78. 116

LEVEL 4: GEOMETRY AND TRIG

79. D
80. D
81. B
82. D
83. 4
84. 48

LEVEL 4: PASSPORT TO ADVANCED MATH

85. B
86. C
87. B
88. A
89. 1
90. 14

LEVEL 4: PROBLEM SOLVING AND DATA

91. C
92. C
93. 5
94. 1.5
95. 4.5
96. 3/4 or .75

LEVEL 5: HEART OF ALGEBRA

97. B
98. B
99. D
100. D
101. 56
102. 46.2

LEVEL 5: GEOMETRY AND TRIG

103. A
104. D
105. 5.54
106. 16
107. 252
108. 216

LEVEL 5: PASSPORT TO ADVANCED MATH

109. C
110. A
111. 4
112. 36
113. 250
114. 5

LEVEL 5: PROBLEM SOLVING AND DATA

115. B
116. C
117. D
118. 3
119. 8.55 or 8.56
120. 5

ACTIONS TO COMPLETE AFTER YOU HAVE READ THIS BOOK

1. **Take another practice SAT**

   You should see a substantial improvement in your score.

2. **Continue to practice SAT math problems for 10 to 20 minutes each day**

   Keep practicing problems of the appropriate levels until two days before the SAT.

3. **Review this book**

   If this book helped you, please post your positive feedback on the site you purchased it from; e.g. Amazon, Barnes and Noble, etc.

4. **Claim your FREE bonuses**

   If you have not done so yet, visit the following webpage and enter your email address to receive additional problems with solutions.

www.thesatmathprep.com/NewSAT2016.html

About the Author

Dr. Steve Warner, a New York native, earned his Ph.D. at Rutgers University in Pure Mathematics in May, 2001. While a graduate student, Dr. Warner won the TA Teaching Excellence Award.

After Rutgers, Dr. Warner joined the Penn State Mathematics Department as an Assistant Professor. In September, 2002, Dr. Warner returned to New York to accept an Assistant Professor position at Hofstra University. By September 2007, Dr. Warner had received tenure and was promoted to Associate Professor. He has taught undergraduate and graduate courses in Precalculus, Calculus, Linear Algebra, Differential Equations, Mathematical Logic, Set Theory and Abstract Algebra.

Over that time, Dr. Warner participated in a five year NSF grant, "The MSTP Project," to study and improve mathematics and science curriculum in poorly performing junior high schools. He also published several articles in scholarly journals, specifically on Mathematical Logic.

Dr. Warner has more than 15 years of experience in general math tutoring and tutoring for standardized tests such as the SAT, ACT and AP Calculus exams. He has tutored students both individually and in group settings.

In February, 2010 Dr. Warner released his first SAT prep book "The 32 Most Effective SAT Math Strategies," and in 2012 founded Get 800 Test Prep. Since then Dr. Warner has written books for the SAT, ACT, GRE, SAT Math Subject Tests and AP Calculus exams.

Dr. Steve Warner can be reached at

steve@SATPrepGet800.com

BOOKS BY DR. STEVE WARNER

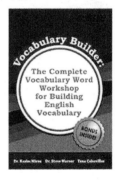

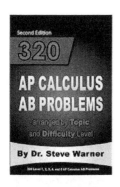

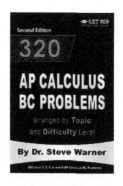

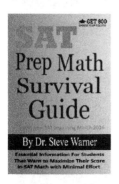

Made in the USA
Middletown, DE
25 February 2022